HEAR ME ROAR

Women,

Motorcycles,

and the

Rapture

of the Road

Ann Ferrar

With Photographs by the Author

A Whirlaway Book
Whitehorse Press
North Conway, New Hampshire

Except where noted, photographs were taken by the author.
Cover design by Tom Lau
Book design by Kay Schuckhart

We recognize that some words, model names and designations
mentioned herein are the property of the trademark holder. We
use them for identification purposes only.

Published by Whitehorse Press
P.O. Box 60
North Conway, New Hampshire 03860-0060
Phone: 603-356-6556 or 800-531-1133
Fax: 603-356-6590
E-mail: CustomerService@WhitehorsePress.com
Web site: www.WhitehorsePress.com

First published by Crown Trade Paperbacks, New York, 1996

ISBN 1-884313-24-8

5   4   3   2   1

Printed in the United States of America

For Frank, with love and thanks

CONTENTS

AUTHOR'S PREFACE:
TO THE NEXT GENERATION

"Ginger Rogers did everything Fred Astaire did. She just did it backward in high heels."

—Ann Richards, motorcyclist, former governor of Texas

On a stretch of open road, somewhere between Mount Rushmore and Sturgis, South Dakota, I found myself in the midst of something that would alter the course of my life. It was an August day back in 1990. I rode with a troupe of women who, to me at the time, looked like goddesses. I had never *seen* women like this: proud and serene at the helms of their own motorcycles, hair blowing with the wind, fringed leather fluttering from clutch grips and jackets and chaps, and all the while, the powerful rumble and roar of about 30 female-driven engines. This striking image emblazoned itself in my consciousness and planted the seed that would become *Hear Me Roar*. It was the start of a six-year journey that took me from coast to coast on my own two wheels, a journey that forced me to challenge my own concept of myself as a 20th century American woman—and, in so doing, to discover my own hidden strengths.

A lot has happened in women's motorcycling since the first printing of *Roar* in 1996. In 1993, midway through my working travels, I'd interviewed a marketing analyst of a major Japanese motorcycle manufacturer, who thought the number of women riding at that time was inflated, because "a lot of young males registered sport bikes in their mothers' names." To that short-sighted analyst I send a paraphrase of a feminist anthem: *We are women, hear us roar, in numbers too big to ignore.* In 1998, J.D. Power and Associates conducted an independent survey of actual motorcycle owners, and found that women now own nearly a quarter of all new motorcycles in the USA. This nearly *triples* registration figures gathered just a few years earlier. Women now comprise more than a third of graduates of the Motorcycle Safety Foundation's Beginning Rider Courses. And you'd better believe that mothers—and grandmothers—are registering their own bikes in their own names, because an American Motorcyclist Association (AMA) survey showed the average age of women riders is 43. In 1997, the AMA held a three-day, national Women & Motorcycling Conference, the first in the organization's long history. The event was so successful, the AMA museum expanded its exhibit devoted to women riders. A second conference was scheduled for 2000.

The motorcycle industry is finally waking up to reality. In 1999, the Buell Motorcycle Company introduced the 500cc Blast, a nimble standard bike aimed at beginning riders and the inseam-challenged. Ironically, the same company that had employed the skeptical analyst recently sent a direct-mail survey to female riders across the nation, asking, "When do you expect to buy a new bike" and "What special offers would influence your purchasing decision?" At the same time, female entrepreneurs have taken the bull by the horns. Women-owned businesses like Femmegear and Mota are designing riding gear for female shapes, while a growing number of web mistresses are creating e-zines and networking portals for their sisters in the wind.

In the midst of these exciting times, the motorcycling community has lost several pioneers. Dot Robinson, legendary sidecar endurance racer and founding member of the Motor Maids, died at the age of 87. Robinson was an elegant, steel-willed iconoclast, outspoken yet ever a lady, and always stellar in her endeavors. If some producer had been smart enough to cast a young Katharine Hepburn as Dot Robinson in the height of her racing career in the 1930s and '40s, the result on the silver screen could have been a classic.

We were saddened by the loss of Fran Crane, who epitomized what I call "existential motorcycling," with her Guinness records for non-stop rides across the American continent on her BMW. Several times Crane competed and placed among the top finishers of the Iron Butt Rally, riding an average of 11,000 miles in 11 straight days. During the 1999 IBR, Crane was involved in an accident and later died. This understated woman was so modest about her accomplishments that she threw out her many trophies. It was never the brass ring or the destination that mattered. Crane found peace and satisfaction in challenging her own limits.

Today, women continue to push their two-wheeling limits in wildly diverse and exhilarating ways. In 1999, at age 66, Ardys Kellerman finished her third Iron Butt, adding a bronze medal to the silver she earned two years earlier. In 1998, New Mexico's Judy Kowalski was one of a group who rode 500cc Royal Enfield Bullets in the steep, winding roads of the Indian Himalayas to reach Khardung La, the highest motorable pass in the world (18,380 feet). Kowalski, fired up by this experience, started her own touring company, WhipTail Motorcycle Adventures, to someday lead other women to the "Top of the World." That same year, Carla King, a San Francisco technical writer, rode across China on a Chang Jiang sidecar motorcycle, dispatching her travelogues on the Internet. In 2000 she tackled India.

Among those on a quest for speed, Angelle Seeling, a 30-year-old New Orleans nurse, has soared to 188.8 mph as a champion NHRA Pro Stock drag racer. Vicky Jackson Bell, 36, a hairstylist, mother, and former motocrosser, is now a speed diva in 125 Grand Prix road racing, while Stephanie "Stevie" Welch is an 18-year-old upstart at the AMA professional dirt track. In just a few short years, the Women's Motocross League has grown from a handful of women into a 3,000-member sports organization.

There were, are, and will be other great riders from the USA and elsewhere who will contribute their own chapters to women's motorcycling history. Germany's Jutta Kleinschmidt has raced on some of the earth's toughest terrain in the Paris-Dakar (Africa) Rally. Brazilian Moniika Vega rode 83,500 miles through 53 countries in 444 days (on a 125 cc bike), earning a Guinness World Record in 1991. Bernarda "Benka" Pulko of Slovenia is circling the world on a BMW 650 in pursuit of a new Guinness record. She plans to be the first woman to ride all seven continents.

The achievements of the women in *Roar,* as determined leaders—as visionaries in some cases—are awesome, as this chronicle of their triumphs attests. In 1993, Sue Slate, Gin Shear and friends rode to the Arctic Circle to raise funds for breast cancer research. In 1996, they spearheaded a huge campaign known as the Pony Express National Ride for Breast Cancer Research, uniting thousands of motorcyclists from diverse backgrounds. Through 1999, the Pony Express raised nearly a million dollars for the cause. The 2000 Pony Express will greatly up the ante, as will future events they are planning.

And so I invite the next generation of motorcycling enthusiasts, and curators of women's and transportation history, to discover their stories and many others within these pages. The greatest legacy of *Hear Me Roar* is that it has preserved, and brought to public light, a little-known facet of women's progression in 20th century America. This legacy has already taken root, as is testified in the many letters I have received from women who were inspired to learn to ride and to join women's motorcycling organizations after reading this book. Their lives were changed— as was mine—once they learned how these dynamic, unusual women just wouldn't take no for an answer.

To date, *Hear Me Roar* still stands as the first and only book of its kind. It is a journalistic chronicle of key women riders, racers, activists and world travelers, written within the larger, historical context of mobility and women's independence. This printing of *Roar* contains an updated Riders' Resource Directory. Think of the directory as a compass pointing to as many roads as you'd like to explore. And when you think of these great women, remember that they chose motorcycling to push through personal barriers, to effect social change—and to savor life to its fullest.

Ann Ferrar

INTRODUCTION

I was riding along a deserted highway in Florida when the Great Nor'easter of March 1993 struck the whole eastern seaboard. I was on my way home to New York. My mount at the time was a sporty, 650cc Hawk GT with no wind protection other than a small, bubble-shaped shield.

Suddenly, the storm rocked the sky. On came the lightning, the wind, and the rain. My bike was precariously top-heavy with camping gear. Leaning against the wind, I struggled to stay on course but some gusts were so violent, at times I was blown across my lane. Just minutes before the power lines went out, I pulled safely into the garage of Teri and Harold, a couple I'd met the week before at my campground.

Farther north, along almost every state on my route, a blizzard was blowing. I couldn't wait for long—I had to get back to my job as a writer for a voluntary health organization. And so I rode into freshly fallen snow and ice along I-95 and sub-zero windchills from North Carolina to Manhattan.

What was I doing on my motorcycle in the dead of winter so far from home? Bike Week, the enormous, yearly convergence of motorcyclists in Daytona Beach, had lured me south. During that trip, I had a variety of experiences that would later enrich this book.

I met the legendary Dot Robinson, an octogenarian astride a Harley who had been a champion sidecar endurance racer. I met a contingent of her Motor Maids, the first

Unsung Heroines: Turning a New Page in Herstory

nationwide club for women riders. I flicked my bike through the winding roads of a state park where oak trees formed a canopy and the only sound was my engine. In town, I cruised Main Street amid the rumble of thousands of Harleys, many ridden by women. At the speedway, I watched the Daytona 200. Every morning I had a breakfast of pancakes and friendly conversation at a campsite where a local BMW club served as hosts. There, I met Teri and Harold.

That's how it is in the world of motorcycling. During my travels, I encountered its various subcultures. People from all walks of life—from yuppies to outlaws—were drawn together in a diverse but definite *community*.

Daytona '93 was the midway point in an

intense six-year odyssey throughout which I interviewed women, shot photographs, and wrote this book. My travels took me and my motorcycles (I've owned four) intermittently from Laconia, New Hampshire, to California, and from Ontario to Key West. My journey started in 1990 en route to the Black Hills Motor Classic in Sturgis, South Dakota, the *other* mega-rally of bikers. In those days, I earned my living as a freelance writer, and I went to Sturgis to write a magazine article about the first all-women Harley drag races.

I was a passenger on a friend's motorcycle, because I hadn't learned to ride yet. Having grown up in New York City taking mass transit, I'd reached my early thirties with little *car* driving experience. The thought of operating a motorcycle was something I couldn't fathom. So I rode on the back because I just loved being on a bike. But the lack of control and dependency on someone else were frustrating.

At Sturgis, I saw more women riding their own motorcycles than I'd ever imagined. My life changed when I met members of a club called Women in the Wind. There was an exuberance and an audacity about them. They were rule breakers and different from any other women I'd known. Their spirited honesty, and their stories of their many adventures and travails on the road, were the initial inspirations for this book.

These women encouraged me to take the bull by the handlebars and learn how to ride. Immediately, I learned the basics at a Motorcycle Safety Foundation course. After that, it took all my nerve to ride in New York City, with its crater-potholes, killer cabs, maniacal bicycle messengers, and hit-me-if-you-dare pedestrians. I survived, and then a sea change occurred in my psyche. The other hassles of life in that difficult city seemed eas-

ier compared to the gauntlet of two-wheeled urban combat, which I'd faced and overcome.

As I spoke to more and more women, I saw similar emotional tread patterns. In so many cases, a woman's mastery of a motorcycle was metaphoric for her ability to surmount other obstacles. I also found that women, as well as men, have played a vital role in the evolution of motorcycling as a slice of American history. Take Adeline and Augusta Van Buren. In 1916, these sisters became the first women to complete a transcontinental trip on two solo motorcycles. They did it to show Uncle Sam that women could serve as motorcycle dispatch carriers during World War I. The Van Burens are gone now, but I had the pleasure of meeting Adeline's daughter, Anne Tully Ruderman, who wrote this tribute to her mother:

> Adeline Van Buren's name is not in the Guinness Book of World Records, nor is it in a Women's Hall of Fame. It ought to be, for she rode and wrote a unique chapter in the story of women's independence. The newspapers called my mother and aunt the gentle sex, but made much of the fact that they had done something no women had ever done, in a manner that no man in his right mind would attempt. They tackled a "daring test," riding into the wilderness, over mountains, and across deserts, without benefits of arms or man.[1]

About three-quarters of a century later, as I roared off on one of my cushy, three-thousand-mile trips on paved roads, I met Bessie B. Stringfield, who had made her mark during World War II. Imagine how many jaws dropped at the sight of this lone black woman riding a Harley for the army!

Joanna Strohn

The author on the road In 1993 with the Honda Hawk GT, Westerville, Ohio

Stringfield, now deceased, was a one-woman civil rights movement.

Today's women motorcyclists are iconoclasts who are doing something totally unexpected of women, yet they are largely unrecognized outside of the motorcycling community. The women in this book include a hair stylist who became the fastest woman on a Harley-Davidson drag bike, a grandmother who rode through the mud and frost heaves of the Canadian Yukon, and a computer programmer and remedial reading teacher who spearheaded a "Pony Express" motorcycle ride around the nation to raise money for breast cancer research.

This book is about diehards who live and breathe their motorcycles, who view their bikes as extensions of their personalities, and who steep themselves in a milieu—be it a disciplined life riveted to racing or a free-spirited lifestyle centered on the Harley "mystique." These women are nonconformists. Each one is doing something that only the tiniest fraction of the United States population is doing. There are, at the highest estimate, only about seven hundred fifty thousand women who ride motorcycles.

When a woman decides to ride, often the act is more than it appears. Ever since the late nineteenth century, when women bucked tra-

Joanne Flaster

On Long Island, New York, with my current bike, a BMW R65

dition to ride bicycles, the sight of a woman awheel has been tied to a slew of conflicting messages about her femininity, competency, power, and liberation. Suffragist Susan B. Anthony was quoted as saying that riding bicycles "did more to emancipate woman than anything else in the world" and that a woman moving forth on two wheels was "the picture of free, untrammelled womanhood."

Today, women bikers are still scrutinized in a way that our male counterparts are not. We're controlling these huge, mechanical beasts, getting them to do our bidding. A few people don't know what to make of the girl-next-door taking charge, breaking free.

Fortunately, for every observer who just doesn't get it, there are two enthusiasts saluting the woman biker with a "thumbs-up."

There were a couple of days in the summer of 1993, when I was humbled to be in the presence of eighty-year-old Vera Griffin, one of the Motor Maids' first officers. For decades, Vera had ridden motorcycles that had to be cranked (kick-started). Most roads she traveled were unpaved. "I called all my motorcycles my magic carpets," she said, "because they took me to wondrous places I could not have gone any other way."

Vera gave me a pile of original vintage photographs and period clippings that helped shape the section about women in the 1930s through the 1950s. I promised to take good care of the photos and return them. But I think Vera sensed something. "Keep them," she said. "What you're doing is very important. I have no one to leave them to."

Vera Griffin passed away seven months later, in the winter of 1994. She had knowingly prepared me to carry on the legacy of an unusual group of women whose contributions to "herstory"—and history—have remained largely hidden.

I now live on eastern Long Island near the beach and great roads, with my other half, Frank Dusek, and our three sets of twins: my 1987 BMW R65 and his 1973 Harley-Davidson Sportster and 1950 Indian Scout. It is eighty years since the Van Burens made their trailblazing journey on machines so primitive, the headlights were lit with matches. I will never be half the rider that they were, or that Vera was. But in my own way, through the gift of story, I hope I have done them proud.

ANN FERRAR

Part 1:
Women, Motorcycles, and the Rapture of the Road

"*I like the speed, the competition. And I love the motorcycle. There's something about this machine that thrills me and I just can't seem to get enough.*"

—Fran Crane, Scotts Valley, California

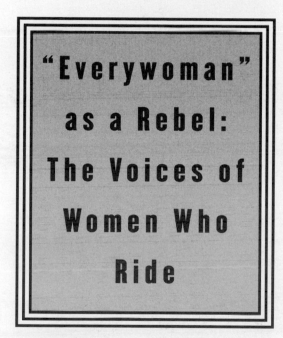

"Everywoman" as a Rebel: The Voices of Women Who Ride

"*I've always been a rebel, your basic tomboy type. Something happens when you put on that black leather jacket and boots. It's like you could kick ass, even though you wouldn't. A certain amount of power comes with it.*"

—Judy Jackson, Toledo, Ohio

"*Riding has given me a lifestyle of my own and a place where I belong. The motorcycle is a stress reliever that helps me block out the corporate bull at work. When I'm eating too big a slice of the system pie, I think about that bike and that part of myself, and it helps me get through the sludge.*"

—Sandy Couture, Toledo, Ohio

"*I felt like that song, 'I am woman, hear me roar!' I can do anything! I can have grandchildren! I can cook! I can ford rivers on a motorcycle!*"

—Catharine Rambeau, Lantana, Florida

"*I was asked to speak at a fundraiser and was introduced as a woman who wears many hats. I said, 'One of my hats is a motorcycle helmet.' People take that as an expression of power and self-confidence. You have to be secure to be a professional woman with a certain standing, and ride a motorcycle.*"

—Ana Dumois, New York City

OPPOSITE: **Cindy Earle with her BMW K75S**

> **"I**'m not a 'biker.' I don't wear black leather with studs. I ski and ride horses. There are parallels. It's the flirting with danger, the idea of pushing my limits within safety factors I can control. Riding a motorcycle is a little more challenging than most people are willing to tackle. Something prevents them from doing it, but I'm *doing it.*"
>
> **—Jenny Alexander,
> Santa Barbara, California**

These are the voices of motorcycling women—a little-known breed of gutsy, independent mavericks who explode convention every time they start their engines. The women above are in their thirties, forties, fifties, and sixties. They ride all types of motorcycles, from a powerful 1000cc BMW sport-tourer, to a raucous 883cc Harley-Davidson Sportster, to a small, springy 250cc Honda dirt bike.

Many of these women have taken physical and emotional risks to get on the front seat. They have challenged personal limits and defied social stereotypes. They have raised eyebrows among family, friends, and coworkers. In so doing, they have carved niches in a male-dominated lifestyle and broken records in a male-dominated sport. They have ridden to the far reaches of the globe and reinvented themselves on motorcycles.

Fran Crane is a parking enforcement officer who is obsessed with bikes and the road. She earned a Guinness Book world record for marathon-riding a BMW K100 from New York to San Francisco in forty-four hours and twenty minutes. Judy Jackson is a nursing student and mother who started riding twenty years ago after a serious lung operation. For Jackson, it was therapy, "a way to get back among the living." Catharine Rambeau is a magazine editor and grandmother who rode the little dirt bike on a solo, 14,300-mile trip from the United States to the southern tip of Argentina—to Ushuaia, a village on the island of Tierra del Fuego known as the end of the world. She was the first woman ever to do so. Sandy Couture escapes from her office on the Sportster. She is a "lifestyle biker" in a subculture where the world revolves around Harleys, leather, and chrome.

Jenny Alexander is an educational psychologist who sees herself as "fairly traditional,

Fran Crane on her K100RS, similar to the bike she rode into the record books

A moment of female pride: Members of the Lady Hawks Motorcycle Club of Maryland show off their trophies for participation in various events.

and yet I ride a motorcycle. It's unexpected. That's part of the kick." Cindy Earle is a schoolteacher who spends summers on her bike. Cuban émigré Ana Dumois is a Ph.D. who heads an agency that provides health care to underprivileged women. She rides to poor communities astride a weathered, 450cc Honda Rebel because "we are not in a box. We are open, accessible. We are about people taking their destinies into their own hands and taking risks to promote change. My riding a motorcycle represents all that."

Indeed, it does. Today's motorcycling women are a legion well over half a million strong—roughly a tenfold increase from the 1960s. And yet they are still just a fraction of the nation's 7.5 million motorcycle riders.

Who are these women?

They are wives, mothers, grandmothers, white-collar professionals, athletes, and blue-collar workers. About a third have a college background or degree. They are lawyers, secretaries, corporate vice presidents, small-business owners, and homemakers. They range in age from teenagers to octogenarians. A few are celebrities—actresses Ann-Margret and Kirstie Alley, tennis greats Martina Navratilova and Gabriela Sabatini, and singers k. d. lang, Wynonna Judd, Tanya Tucker, and Queen Latifa are among the glitterati-on-wheels. Others are dignitaries, such as former Texas governor Ann Richards, who learned to ride a Harley in celebration of her sixtieth birthday. While the majority of women motorcyclists are caucasian and heterosexual, women of color and lesbian riders are more visible than in decades past.

Like their male peers, women riders of all backgrounds have a passion for two wheels that is fueled by many factors: the exhilaration of the motorcycle's wind-in-the-face freedom, coupled with a strong sense of independence and control; the allure of adventure and the closeness with nature; the kinesthetic relationship with a responsive machine that is straddled and ridden like a horse; the camaraderie of the motorcycle community; and the mystique, the romanticism, the challenges around every bend in the road.

> "It's the blump-blump-blump of the engine. It goes with your heartbeat. Then there's the sound of the pipes. On one level, it gets down to real primitive stuff. On a conscious level, I have freedom waiting in my garage."
>
> —Sandy Couture

> "I feel a cowgirl spirit. On a bike, you're one with the elements like the old cowboys were. That's part of what our country was founded on. It's a real closeness with life."
>
> —Jacquie Bonney, rancher, dirt bike and rodeo rider, Pueblo, Colorado

For many women, the bike represents all of these things. Often, it becomes a vehicle of self-discovery. For some, it conveys rebellion.

To sixty-four-year-old Ana Dumois, rebellion isn't new—her motorcycle is merely an extension of her nature. In the 1950s, Dumois was involved in the Cuban revolution. She said, "When Castro betrayed democracy, I left Cuba. I chose my current profession because I knew it would be tough and I love a good fight!"

In her quest to help underprivileged women, Dumois chose a motorcycle to overthrow the image of the stodgy executive. "When I ride to one of our clinics, I don't show up in a fancy dress in a big car," she explained. "I am the director, but the staff and clients can relate to me. You have to be different to promote change."

Rebels come in all shapes and sizes. They can be found among the conservative Motor Maids, the nation's first club for women riders, founded in 1940. At their conventions, many gray-haired members still parade in their matching uniforms through small-town America. And there are rebels among a group of leather-bustiered, thigh-high-booted women who cruise Main Street during Daytona Bike Week, a motorcycle Mardi Gras. Their club patch screams, CUNTILEROS. And there are rebels among the quiet individualists who are seriously obsessed with bikes, like endurance rider Fran Crane. "My mother threatened to disown me if she so much as caught me on the *back* of a motorcycle," said Crane. "So I started riding because she didn't want me to. Today, I don't go anywhere in four-wheeled vehicles." Crane, now forty-nine, has owned twenty-

Ana Dumois on her 1991 Harley-Davidson FXR, one of three bikes she owns. In the boardroom of her agency is a wall of plaques: her diplomas, citations, distinguished service awards . . . and in the middle, "Long Distance Female, Big Country Moto Guzzi Rally, 1986."

Becky Brown

Sandy Couture on her 1990 Sportster, an 883cc Hugger. Drag pipes let the neighbors know she's coming home. She says, "I believe in the cliche 'Loud pipes save lives.' Plus I like having a macho bike!"

eight bikes and logged many hundreds of thousands of miles.

METAMORPHOSIS

When a woman masters a motorcycle, often she undergoes a change that spreads to other aspects of her life. This growth doesn't come from merely donning a leather jacket and boots. Some women take a long look at themselves, accept self-imposed challenges, and make changes with great resolve. When they learn to control a motorcycle, they do likewise with their fate.

Sandy Couture, a divorcée from Toledo, Ohio, moved to the front seat when she was thirty-four. "Riding my own bike has changed my life forever and I love every bit of it," she declared. "Before I bought my own bike, I'd been a passenger on Harleys for fifteen years. I was proud to be a biker, but I always had problems with the thinking that a biker woman 'belonged' to her man. I was no militant women's libber, but I couldn't live with the double standards."

She couldn't live with the local biker scene, either: "It seemed like every time my husband would say, 'Let's go for a ride,' he'd get in the wind five yards to the nearest bar and talk about what a biker he was."

After her divorce, Couture said, "I was frustrated on the back of a guy's bike, praying I'd get home okay because he'd had too much to drink. They took you for a ride and then expected you to put out. I refused to go through it."

In 1990, when she bought her Harley Sportster, she found freedom and a new circle of friends. A year later she was elected Toledo chapter president of the motorcycle club Women in the Wind.

Like many beginners, Couture had early doubts. "At first I wondered, Hey, can you really do this? It had been a long time since I'd had to work so hard to overcome the fear

> "When I turned forty-two, my husband decided to leave and 'find himself.' For twenty-four years, he was all I had. In an effort to claim my independence, I decided to ride my own bike. Because I'm only five feet one and ninety-five pounds, some people thought I would never be able do it. My dream of being in control of this machine made me even more determined. My life has gotten better for all the self-worth and perseverance riding has taught me. My work, too, has reflected my strong sense of accomplishment."
>
> **—Nikki Mongaraz, former secretary promoted to computer software trainer, Frankfort, Illinois[1]**

> "When I was younger, I did the domestic part of my life. Now I can be proud of what I accomplish on my own. A lot of women never experience this because they don't get the opportunity to go on the road alone. I didn't when traveling with my husband; he used to take care of me. But now, on the road by myself, it's me, the motorcycle, and that's it."
>
> **—Cindy Earle, fifty-something, Baton Rouge, Louisiana**

of something. But once I mastered it, I knew I could do anything I put my mind to."

Couture's path to self-realization followed a familiar pattern. Dagmar O'Connor, Ph.D., a New York psychologist and author, commented: "If you take a physical or emotional risk, you break through a barrier. This usually has a ripple effect into other areas. Especially if a woman sees the motorcycle as a dare—something she was afraid of—overcoming it can provide the confidence to tackle things she might fear emotionally. Physical risks often become symbols and practice grounds for emotional risks."

Vicki Randle, singer-percussionist for the band on *The Tonight Show with Jay Leno*, rode dirt bikes as a West Coast teenager. Today, at forty-one, she says, "I spend a lot of time commuting on the freeways. When I arrive at the studio after being on my Harley, I feel so good."

"*Riding is intuitive. On a bike, you're invisible to cars, so you have to be aware of your surroundings at all times. You're aware of your speed, how you lean, the condition of the bike—you become part of that machine and it becomes a part of you. It's total involvement.*"

—Vicki Randle, musician, Venice, California

THE REVERIE OF THE ROAD

The road calls. The bike beckons, like a stabled horse that needs to be taken out. Whether it's the deep, loud rumble of a Harley, the clickety-clack of a BMW twin, or the turbinelike drone of a high-revving Japanese sport bike, the speed, motion, and machinery orchestrate their own mellifluous song. With the wind rushing past her body and the steady roar of the machine below, all of the rider's senses are engaged in a hyperreceptive mode. She is alert yet relaxed, absorbed in a moving meditation. On the road, at speed, the mind is cleared of rubble. Her concentration is so focused, she is nothing but the sum of her experience and her awareness of the present.

The view from the saddle is panoramic, unobstructed by the TV-tube frame of a car windshield. She marvels at the scenery . . . and may be simultaneously splattered with it. She is undeniably alive, connected at once to her own humanity, to the earth, and to the powerful bike that carries her faster and farther than she could go on her own. On top of her two-wheeled flying machine, the rider downshifts and banks into curves with authority. She upshifts to fifth on a straightaway . . . and with a twist of the throttle, she's as free as a woman can be on the ground.

In her autobiography, *On the Perimeter*,[2] the late Hazel Kolb wrote, "The bike is strapping like a bull, sleek like a running horse, and has the kind of power that, when you yank on it, makes your eyes slide to the horizon and your imagination fly beyond." Kolb was a Motor Maid and grandmother who swapped her leisure suit for a leather jacket. She left small-town Missouri in 1979 to circumnavigate the United States on a Harley. With those words, Kolb captured the exuberance of a woman rider soaring above the rote of daily existence. A woman riding a motorcycle is buoyant, both metaphorically and in a very tangible way. On her bike, she is whole, not fragmented as so many women are when catering to children, husbands, lovers, and bosses. When she's riding, the constantly changing ground beneath her wheels is her own private space. She is mobile—no one can catch her. She can't be squished into any of the compartments that women are forced to inhabit.

Karen Signell, Ph.D., author of *Wisdom of the Heart: Working with Women's Dreams,* observed: "Women have been held back so much. We are grounded in careful realities. We do these unending tasks. We do the dishes and then we do them again. We cook meals and then we cook them again. Riding a motorcycle provides the thrill of moving forward. A lone woman breaking through barriers and showing what she can do is inspiring. It's also true for a great skier or a woman who can fly a plane or race a horse. She captures our imagination."

The woman who gets on a motorcycle has to *really want* to

Courtesy American Woman Motorscene

Courtney Caldwell of *American Woman Motorscene*

ride. She knows that on the bike, she may bake in the dry heat of a desert highway . . . or shiver from the chill of a thunderstorm that dumps buckets of hail and fogs her helmet visor so badly, the road becomes a blur. In city traffic, her mind revs as fast as the engine. She maneuvers the bike aggressively yet defensively, making hundreds of split-second decisions per mile, upon which her safety—her life—depends. Sometimes the machine breaks down. She is vulnerable. She is not surrounded by four doors and a roof. She resorts to her own devices and, sometimes, the helpfulness of other bikers who miraculously appear on the side of the road. The Everywoman who gets on a motorcycle drinks in all these experiences, which just don't happen in a four-wheeled "cage."

A CROSSROADS AT THIRTY-SOMETHING

Courtney Caldwell, publisher of *American Woman Motorscene* magazine, noted that many women are ready to embrace the challenges of the road on two wheels when they reach their mid-thirties—when they've matured, when their careers are established and the children are in school. Said Caldwell, "By the age of thirty-five, women are more secure about who they are and they're looking for ways to vent their adventurous side." Caldwell views the recent surge in women riding motorcycles as an extension of the fact that more women are enjoying action-adventure sports, from skydiving to rock climbing.

"More women are in management positions, where there's risk and stress," she pointed out. "As men do, they're seeking ways to relieve stress and they believe, 'If I can do this in my career, then I can ride a motorcycle.' Adventurous and challenging sports are a new frontier."

For some gay women, the motorcycle can be a visible symbol that tells the world, "This is who I am."

> "I'm a thirty-nine-year-old woman who happens to be gay. I joined Women on Wheels and had the good fortune to meet some great straight women who accept me and my partner just the way we are. You might want to know it works both ways. It does get a bit tiresome when you married women get too long-winded about your husbands. Some of us have survived on our own. Some of us have worked hard to buy our own motorcycles, which feels pretty darn good."
>
> —Shelly Beeson, Seattle, Washington[3]

> **"I** prefer to be around women who are like me. I'd rather not hear straight women say they have to get home from a ride, pick up the kids, and do the dishes because Bob has been out all day and he doesn't want to do it. I perceive that generally, dyke bikers are more self-sufficient. They'll say, 'My bike broke and I've got to fix it.' A lot of straight women say, 'Honey, my bike is leaking oil.'"

—L. B. Gunn, thirty-four, Women's Motorcycle Contingent organizer, San Francisco, California

L. B. Gunn

AN INVASION OF WANNA-BES

"Riding a motorcycle is like an Annie Oakley thing," said Sandy Couture. "When they first settled the West, women had to have guts and not be prissy little frail things. That is what it takes to ride a bike. You have to get your manicure dirty."

That's the difference between real women motorcyclists and the cadre of fashion models and movie and TV stars who began decking themselves in studded leather in the early to mid-1990s. Women riders spawned a motorcycle fashion and image craze that invaded popular culture. Trend watchers called it biker chic.

"Motorcycle mania brought black leather as much into the fashion vernacular as the little black dress," tolled *Harper's Bazaar* as designers put models ("prissy little frail things") on motorcycles in TV and print ads. The Council of Fashion Designers of America presented an award to Harley-Davidson MotorClothes for what *Newsweek* dubbed "decades of style influence on everyone from club kids to Chanel." Stars dressed like bikers to prove they still "had it." Marking her sixtieth birthday in a 1992 issue of *Life,* a leathered-up Liz Taylor straddled her purple Harley named Passion. Comedienne Roseanne, sporting a new tattoo and a biker jacket, vamped for the cover of *Us.*

More and more images of attractive, independent women at the controls have appeared continuously throughout the media. And yet, despite all the hype, a real woman riding a motorcycle down Main Street, USA, is still a curiosity. She triggers reactions that range from awe and smiles of approval to frowns of disdain or even fear.

> **"I** see expressions of awe in little girls. But some adults don't know what to think. One time, a friend and I pulled up next to a pair of seniors at a stoplight. As soon as they heard our bikes, we heard their door locks go click, click! We just laughed."
>
> **—Becky Brown, factory worker and mother, Toledo, Ohio**

At rest stops, complete strangers are drawn to the woman who's just pulled in on a motorcycle. People wonder what kind of person she is. On the road, with her dark sunglasses, leather jacket, and boots, a weekday careerwoman/weekend biker may be perceived as anything from a goddess on wheels or a sex fantasy, to a tomboy or an outlaw biker "mama." B movies like *Chopper Chicks in Zombietown* and *She-Devils on Wheels* have perpetuated such myths.

As this book will show, motorcycling women have been doing something bold and unconventional for nearly a hundred years—long before the fashion mavens, the celebrity wanna-bes, and the Madison Avenue media barrage. Women riders are doers, not followers. They are a little-known sorority that has defied gender stereotypes ever since the first motorcycles were rolled out at the turn of the century. Women riders blasted through the mores of Victorianism. They exploded the boundaries of female containment in the 1950s. They predated the modern women's movement. And they have ridden roads less traveled ever since.

So. Who are these two-wheeling women? Some view themselves as *bikers* and partake of a lifestyle where Harleys reign amid leather and chrome.

Others never use the word *biker*, but think of themselves as "motorcyclists" or just people who like to ride. For these women, any brand of bike will do because they each have their own appeal.

Some ride through male resistance; most ride with male encouragement.

Some ride with clubs, attend motorcycle rallies and races, and become involved in motorcycle events to benefit charities and political causes.

> **"I** n Brooklyn, I faced a couple in a car waiting to make a left turn. The woman seemed oppressed or emotionally distraught. As I rode by, she smiled and blew me a kiss. She probably thought, Power to you, you're free. Many times while riding I see in women a look of longing. Perhaps they feel that they, too, might do it someday."
>
> **—Ana Dumois**

Judy Jackson with her Honda Shadow 500

Others ride great distances alone, using their motorcycles as vehicles to explore the world and the limits of their own endurance.

Some ride street bikes on paved roads. Others are dual-sport or off-road jockeys, kicking up dust on desert and mountain trails.

Some are athletes who thrive on speed and competition, while others are weekend cruisers seeking relaxation and camaraderie.

Yet no matter how diverse their backgrounds, and no matter how entrenched they are or aren't in any of motorcycling's subcultures, strong running threads unite women riders. They have invented their own brand of feminism and redefined what is feminine. Like their counterparts in other action-adventure sports, these audacious women have rejected the notion that feminine strength is a contradiction in terms.

"Most women riders are a breed in themselves," said Judy Jackson. "We share a lot of the same views. It's been real good for me, the camaraderie. I don't know if it's that we're tomboys or just terribly independent."

Becky Brown, who founded Women in the Wind, a nationwide club with six hundred members, put it even more simply: "It's part of the whole progression of women. Voting, working, riding motorcycles. More freedom."

CHAPTER TWO

"The motorcycle girl is a twentieth-century phenomenon, but the spirit that moves her is as old as Eve. It was the spirit of the motorcycle girl that sent the pioneer mothers out over the prairies. . . . But it has almost nothing to do with being a perfect lady."

—from *Listen, World!*, a 1925
Hearst newspaper essay

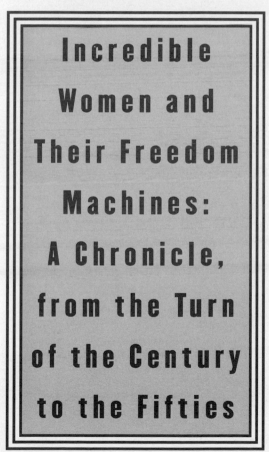

Incredible Women and Their Freedom Machines: A Chronicle, from the Turn of the Century to the Fifties

Today's motorcycling women come from a long line of mavericks who thumbed their noses at convention, hitched up their Victorian skirts, and shocked society by riding bicycles. To ride "the wheel," women dumped their corsets and curfews. They reveled in mobility— and the freedom that comes with it.

Even temperance leader Frances E. Willard, one of the most influential women of the Victorian era, saw bicycling as a symbol of liberation. In 1895, she wrote: "That which made me succeed with the bicycle was precisely what had gained me a measure of success in life—it was the hardihood of Spirit that led me to begin, the persistence of will that held me to my task, and the patience that was willing to begin again when the last stroke had failed."[1]

Six years later, Willard's sentiments would

OPPOSITE: **Motor Maid Vera Griffin of Indiana**

(Vera Griffin Collection)

Two women prepare to hit the road in 1914 on a two-speed Harley-Davidson Model 10-F with a sidecar.

apply to the women who rode the first American-made motorcycles, really gasoline-powered bicycles. Though the motorcycle had been invented in Germany in 1885, it wasn't until 1901 that E. R. Thomas sold the first ones in the United States, followed soon after by Indian, Harley-Davidson, Henderson, Excelsior, and many others.

To appreciate the hardiness of early women riders, one must realize that in the decades before World War II, motorcycles were primitive, persnickety machines, and that our nation was barely strung together by mudways and dirtways. In 1906, the transconti-

nental ride of W. C. Chadeayne, a male biker, was chronicled by a reporter who wrote:

As one penetrates the interior of the American continent, well-made roads give place to almost indistinguishable tracks, often impassable. The desert gives way to mountains, their narrow paths strewn with boulders, over which it is necessary to pick one's way laboriously. Streams and torrents must be plunged through boldly, for bridges are unknown. Such is a brief description of the difficulties that must be faced by the man who is sufficiently intrepid to cross the American continent in this way.[2]

Or the *women* who were sufficiently intrepid—and there were many. In fact, women not only rode motorcycles, they raced and won in competition.

In October 1910, an eighteen-year-old named Clara Wagner rode a four-horsepower motorcycle in a 365-mile endurance race from Chicago to Indianapolis. Even plagued by inclement weather and roads buried in mud, Wagner achieved a perfect score, defeating most of the men. The Federation of American Motorcyclists (the predecessor of today's American Motorcyclist Association) declared Wagner's victory "unofficial" and denied her a trophy.[3]

Five years later, the daughter-mother duo of Effie and Avis Hotchkiss achieved a per-

In 1915, Avis Hotchkiss watched her daughter Effie christen the Pacific with Atlantic Ocean water they carried in the sidecar from New York.

Courtesy Adeline's daughter, Anne Tully Ruderman

Adeline and Augusta Van Buren made a stop at the Akron, Ohio, headquarters of the Firestone Tire Company in 1916.

sonal victory over the continent. It was 1915, a year after the outbreak of World War I. Effie had been working on Wall Street. According to the *New York Sun,* the "rush and clatter and monotony and tension" began to wear on her nerves, so she bought a Harley. She learned to repair it and attached a sidecar. With her mother, Avis, she embarked on a circuitous, five-thousand-mile journey to see the Panama-Pacific International Exposition in San Francisco. Three months later, the Hotchkisses rode the sidecar rig onto the beach and christened the Pacific with a jar of

Atlantic Ocean water they'd carried with them. They rode back to New York and were the first known women to make a round-trip, transcontinental motorcycle journey alone.

The following year, America was still in the midst of a national preparedness movement for the war. Two sisters in their twenties from Brooklyn, New York, left home on Independence Day 1916, each riding her own Indian Power Plus motorcycle. Augusta and Adeline Van Buren were descendants of former president Martin Van Buren. Like the Hotchkisses, their destination was California,

Adeline (left) and Augusta had mudguards installed on their three-speed Indians.
Like gaslamps, the headlights were lit with matches.

Courtesy Anne Tully Ruderman

The Van Burens went to Mexico before riding to California. They were never called to military service. Adeline went to NYU law school and earned her juris doctor. Augusta became an aviatrix and flew well into her sixties.

but they had a larger mission: to prove that women were fit to serve as dispatch riders for the military. Adeline, an English teacher, and Augusta, a business school correspondent, were well prepared for the challenge. They were small-boned "society girls," but they were also award-winning athletes who swam, skated, wrestled, sprinted, and rode horses. Adeline designed their red leather coats, worn with leather caps, breeches, and leggings. Their "masculine uniforms" attracted reporters— and the police, who arrested them several times in small towns between Chicago and the Rockies. In each case, they were released with a

reprimand and shooed out of town.

None of this dampened their enthusiasm. In Colorado, they rode their cycles up the treacherous paths to the summit of Pikes Peak, becoming the first women to drive motorized vehicles up the 14,109-foot mountain. According to one account, in the desert between Denver and Salt Lake, "the deep sands, washes, and rocky trails caused repeated spills, and great physical and mental stamina in rescuing the machines from sink holes and ruts." With their canteens nearly dry, the Van Burens got lost for seven hours in the desert, described as "the most inhospitable and difficult stretch of country in the North American continent."

Nevertheless, for much of the trek during stopovers they had a "bully time." After sixty days and fifty-five hundred meandering miles, the sisters arrived in California, entering history as the first women to make a transcontinental journey on two solo motorcycles. Augusta wrote:

That preparedness pays is demonstrated in the fact that we arrived in San Francisco without having encountered any serious trouble, and with New York air still in our tires. The whole trip was a perilous one for two girls alone. It had its hazards, but it had its pleasures, too, and it all goes to prove that woman "can if she will."

That same year, the Harley-Davidson Motor Company began publication of its *Enthusiast* magazine. It was peppered with the feats of motorcycling women, including the Van Burens, the Hotchkisses, and many others. It was clear that motorcycling women were an independent lot. They broke gender barriers and scored magnificent firsts alongside and, in some cases, well before women in other walks of life. The Hotchkisses had made their extraordinary journey seven years before

Amelia Earhart took her first solo, domestic airplane flight, and five years before women in all states could vote. Curiously, there is no evidence in feminist "herstory" books about the achievements of these unusual iconoclasts, motorcycling women.

THE TWENTIES: HEAR THEM ROAR

In motorcycle terms, never was a nickname for a decade so apt as the Roaring Twenties. The not-for-profit American Motorcyclist Association (AMA) was founded in 1924 to organize social and competitive events, including "Gypsy Tours," large group rides from which most other organized motorcycle rides have

The Harley-Davidson Enthusiast

November, 1929

Vivian Bales, "The Enthusiast Girl"

Courtesy Dot Robinson

Sidecar endurance champion Dot Robinson. "It was hard for some men to accept a woman beating them at their own sport," she said. But when they tried to bar her from racing in the thirties, "no man would say he was afraid of a woman, so they had to let me in."

evolved. The AMA chartered riding clubs. As Henry Ford's automobiles became the nation's preferred means of practical transport, motor-cycling became a sport and a pastime. But it wasn't for everyone—even at this early stage,

because of a few bad apples, the sport had an image problem. One newspaper huffed over "motorcycle speed artists" who "chase up hills at reckless speed, kick up dirt, run over dogs, and make themselves obnoxious."

Beyond motorcycling, the decade conjures up images of social abandon and the unblushing flapper. It was in the twenties that the first Miss America was crowned. But the larger reality was much less glamorous for most women. According to *Second to None: A Documentary History of American Women:*

Neither the war nor the much-vaunted revolution in manners and morals altered the societal expectation that after marriage, the normal American woman would devote herself to domesticity, living a life not far removed from that of her mother. . . . Modern young women increasingly rebelled against the view that marriage was incompatible with a career, though in the absence of an active feminist movement, few met with success in attempting to live out that credo.[4]

In the summer of 1929, right before the stock market crash, a young woman named Vivian Bales (later Faison) defined her own personal credo as "wanderlust or something." She wrote to Harley-Davidson, detailing her dream of riding a five-thousand-mile loop from her home in Georgia, up through the Midwest, and on to the Harley factory in Milwaukee, Wisconsin. Harley officials recognized the public-relations value of putting a woman on a motorcycle. They sponsored Bales, while local dealers provided meals and lodging, over the occasional protests of some disapproving wives. A newsreel company picked up the story of this flapper-on-wheels who sang Betty Boop songs at civic halls along her route. Upon her much-trumpeted arrival in Milwaukee, Bales was awarded a loving cup and dubbed "The Enthusiast Girl." She was the personification of Miss America on a motorcycle.

It was also in the late 1920s that two distinguished women—an Australian-American in Saginaw, Michigan, and an African-American in Boston, Massachusetts—climbed aboard their first motorcycles. Though they were contemporaries, their paths rarely, if ever, crossed. These two women, as much as any prominent male peer, would define the sport of motorcycling for generations to come. Their names, respectively, were Dorothy "Dot" Goulding Robinson and Bessie B. Stringfield.

Dot Robinson and Bessie Stringfield, arguably more than any other riders of their gender, served as inspirations for thousands of women who would follow in their tire tracks. They both loved Harleys, and they both rode great distances under adverse conditions. But their personal styles were very different, as were the obstacles they faced and overcame.

Dot Robinson: A Rebel in (a Pink) Disguise

If Norman Rockwell had depicted a multi-generational motorcycling family, it might

Courtesy Dot Robinson

Dot (right) with her daughter, Betty Robinson Fauls, out for a spin in their Motor Maids uniforms, circa 1940s.

have been the extended clan of Dot Robinson. She was practically born in a side-car made by her father, Jim Goulding. She was sixteen and working as a bookkeeper in Goulding's Saginaw Harley franchise when a motorcyclist named Earl Robinson came in for a quart of oil and was smitten by the spunky, red-haired Dot. They married in 1931, bought the franchise from her father, and moved it to Detroit.

Dot's views may have been influenced by this nuclear family milieu, but she has always been a paradox. While she painted her Harleys pink, wore pink outfits, and attached a lipstick holder to her bike, this woman was tough—yet always in her own relentlessly polite way. She made a religion out of projecting a "lady-like" image, but beneath the perfectly powdered nose and hair-sprayed coif, she was far from a traditional wife and mother.

Beginning in the Depression years, when motorcycles were a "hard-times alternative" to cars, Robinson spent countless weekends competing with men in endurance races throughout the Great Lakes area backcountry. At five feet two, she couldn't touch both feet to the uneven ground in the woods, so she raced in the sidecar classes, carrying a male passenger. She won her first trophy in a hundred-mile race with a perfect score. But the truest test of her skill and perseverance was the arduous, two-day Jack Pine Enduro.

The Enthusiast gave a blow-by-blow account of the 1937 Jack Pine, and concluded: "It was indeed a survival of the fittest and proved beyond any doubt the courage of the riders. Out of 88 entries, only 41 finished the nightmare of sand, swamp, fire lanes and river crossings along the grueling, 500-mile course."

Dot Robinson not only finished, she placed *second* in her class. In 1940, she won. Robinson triumphed over the difficult course and over men who felt she'd invaded their turf. In the late thirties, when former AMA secretary E. C. Smith tried to bar women from competing in the Jack Pine, everyone knew the rule was aimed at Dot. Undaunted, she got AMA members to sign petitions disallowing Smith's rule. Robinson broke this gender barrier three decades before Shirley Muldowney convinced the National Hot Rod Association to let her drag-race a car in 1966. Up until her retirement from competition in 1971, Robinson collected hundreds of trophies for first-place and top-three finishes in various types of endurance events.

Away from the competitive arena, Robinson was ahead of her time as well. From Day One, she managed the books of the Harley franchise, of which she was part owner. In 1940, she became an equal business partner with her husband, Earl, when she bought out their third partner. During World War II, when millions of civilian women

Motor Maids founder Linda Allen Dugeau (left) met Dot in Yosemite for a "girls only" camping trip in 1946.

Vera Griffin Collection

Courtesy Dot Robinson

Dot in 1991 at age seventy-nine. She still drives her husband around in a sidecar. "On a bike," she said, "you're a master of whatever you do. I found that out very young."

worked on war-plant assembly lines, to stay on her bike, Dot took a job as a motorcycle courier for a private defense contractor.

In the late 1930s, Robinson became involved with the Motor Maids, the first nationwide club for women riders. The Motor Maids were the brainchild of a Wellesley College graduate named Linda Allen Dugeau, who envisioned the group as motorcycling's version of the 99s, Amelia Earhart's elite club for women pilots. In search of members who were "neat, clean and above reproach," Dugeau wrote to dealerships around the country. She met Robinson and, together, the pair took three years to locate fifty women. The Motor Maids received their

AMA charter in 1940 and were dedicated to volunteerism and to promoting a positive image of the sport. Robinson was elected their first president and held the position for a quarter century.

While Earl stayed home, Dot hit the road, sometimes clocking as many as fifty thousand miles a year traveling to Motor Maids events and drumming up publicity. Her daughter, Betty, and her mother, Mary, were her frequent companions on the road. Mary rode tandem or in the sidecar. When Betty was very young, Dot strapped the tot behind her with a belt.

When she was sixteen and riding her own bike, Betty accompanied her mother on an eleven-thousand-mile trip around the United States. Said Dot: "I knew that soon, Betty would be old enough to get married and we'd lose her. I wanted her to see the country." She added: "I've had a unique relationship with my daughter all her life. We've had the same thing in common, which means I never had one minute of trouble with her." Over the years, as they rode from state to state in their impeccably pressed Motor Maids uniforms—gray serge with blue trim, matching caps, white boots, and gloves—they became motor-cycling's most famous mother-daughter duo.

Even while wiping Jack Pine mud off her cheeks, Dot took great pride in being the near-perfect lady. "I've always tried to project the best image from a motorcycle," she said. "I made people realize that not all of us are like the bearded, black-leather-jacketed hoods that the media tars us with. Probably my best con-tribution to motorcycling has been my image."

As an octogenarian, Dot has continued to ride. Having totaled more than one and a half million miles on thirty-five Harleys, Robinson has often been called the First Lady of Motorcycling. But she was never called a rabble-rouser. "I didn't go against tradition," she explained. "I got my way with finesse. We have our own ideas, and when somebody tries to force you to do something, and you don't, they say you're rebellious. But you're not, really. You're just being an individual."

Bessie B. Stringfield: The Color Blue

A woman who could have written a book on individualism was Bessie B. Stringfield. She was a legend who embodied what it means to

Bessie B. Stringfield on one of the twenty-seven Harleys she owned in her lifetime.

Bessie B. Stringfield Collection

**"I just crank up a Harley and it talks to me," Stringfield said.
"In my mind, it was the only motorcycle ever made."**

live and breathe a lifetime in the saddle of a motorcycle. Accessible, vulnerable, Stringfield personified the strength and resiliency of a woman who refused to let barriers—either gender based or racial—keep her down. She rode, alone, through an era and through areas where it was considered not just "unladylike" for a woman to ride a bike, but even shocking, perhaps, for a black woman.

Stringfield's beginnings were far less idyllic than Robinson's. Bessie's Dutch caucasian mother died while she was still an infant. Her father, a Jamaican of African descent, abandoned her when she was only five. Although she was adopted by a wealthy Irish couple in Boston, as a young wife and mother, Stringfield was devastated when three children by her first husband died of illness. This tragic loss contributed to Bessie's resolve to lead an independent life. She married and divorced six times.

Even as a girl, Stringfield was fiercely independent. Her adoptive parents gave their blessing to her desire to see the country in her own determined way. When she was sixteen, she said, "I wanted a motorcycle, and I got it." She had no idea how to ride.

"I wrote letters to the Man Upstairs, Jesus Christ," Stringfield recalled. "I put the letters under my pillow and He taught me. One night in my sleep, I saw myself shifting gears and riding around the block. When I got out on the street, that's just what I did!"

Her first bike was a 1928 Indian Scout. It wasn't long before she was riding in situations where most of us wouldn't dare—in stunt shows, for instance. She once rode the Indian around the walls of a carnival motordrome, a huge wooden sphere where the rider uses body language, speed, momentum, and centrifugal force to keep the bike from crashing to the bottom.

In 1930, she replaced the Indian with her first Harley, a Sixty-One. When she was just nineteen, she set out on the first of her solo, cross-country tours, which typically lasted from April to October. "I'd toss a penny over a map, and wherever it landed, I'd go," she said. "I was never afraid on the road because I had the Man Upstairs with me."

Throughout her journeys, Stringfield continued stunt riding whenever opportunities arose. She lay down on the bike and drove, rode sidesaddle, stood on one footpeg, and hoisted herself from one side of the bike to the other.

Her lone adventures were a far cry from "The Enthusiast Girl's" police-escorted, factory-sponsored tour, and the reception she received was hardly on a par with Dot Robinson's experiences. Stringfield traveled with only a leather jacket, a money belt, and whatever spare clothes fit in her saddlebags. "I'd sleep on my Harley at gas stations at night," she recalled. "When I found black folks, I'd sleep next to their children because no one would rent me a motel room."

Stringfield had many positive and happy encounters as well. "All along the way, wherever I rode, the people were overwhelmed to see a Negro woman riding a motorcycle," she said. One time, a Southern white gas station owner was so impressed with her audacity, he filled her fuel tanks, wished her luck, and refused to take any money, saying, "You can just have that little bit of gas!"

After her adoptive parents died in the late 1930s, Stringfield made Miami, Florida, her home base—and promptly raised eyebrows by tooling around the streets standing on the saddle of her Harley. Sometimes she had "co-riders"—her poodles, Sabu and Rodney, perched atop each knee, their front paws on the handlebars. "They thought they were driving," she chuckled.

Some neighborhood people had trouble adjusting to this outspoken woman, her motorcycle, and her dogs, so Stringfield sought the help of a local police captain, Robert Jackson, whom she affectionately called Captain Jack.

He doubted her abilities at first, saying, "If you want to ride a motorcycle in Miami, do exactly as I tell you." He told her to get her bike up to speed, slide off the back, run and catch it, and get back on. Bessie laughed and replied, "That's all?" She completed the maneuver, earning Captain Jack's respect and friendship.

After the outbreak of World War II, while thousands of women joined the WACS (Women's Army Corp), WAVES (Women Accepted for Volunteer Emergency Service), WASPs (Women's Air Force Service Pilots), and WAFS (Women's Auxiliary Ferrying Squadron), Stringfield joined a little-known branch of the army: the motorcycle dispatch unit. Captain Jack was her instructor.

Stringfield was the only woman in a unit of six other black riders. She had to climb her then-current Harley, a Seventy-Four, up a sandy, ninety-foot hill and make an immediate hairpin turn at the crest. To get the bike across a canal, Stringfield learned to weave a bridge with tree limbs. After training, she took to the courier job with gusto. Between 1941 and 1945, she traversed America's primitive back roads and even swamps with classified documents in her saddlebags.

In the late 1950s, Stringfield attended nursing school and earned a license to become a practical nurse. She started the Iron Horse Motorcycle Club in the Miami suburb of Opa Locka, and bought a house "for motorcycle riders to have fun." Her home became the clubhouse, and her escapades ("I was raisin' the devil on a motorcycle") were popular fodder for the newspapers. The local press dubbed her the Motorcycle Queen of Miami.

Decades after the Iron Horse Motorcycle Club disbanded, Stringfield still wore their blue and white colors. Her home was filled with motorcycling memories. There were five AMA trophies in the living room and den, and dozens of photographs and other memorabilia throughout the house.

The only thing missing was her most recent, beloved Harley, a blue 1978 FLH. In the late 1980s, the bike was badly vandalized in a robbery attempt, and Stringfield could not afford to repair it. She sold it and took short rides on borrowed or rented Harleys. She even considered selling her house to buy a new FLHTC. "It's got to be blue and it's got to be new," she said, adding: "I never bought anything used—except husbands!"

In 1990, when she was seventy-nine, the AMA honored Stringfield at the opening of its Heritage Museum in Ohio. Tiny at less than five feet tall, Stringfield peered up at an exhibit that featured her name and likeness. She had twenty-seven Harleys, sixty-three years of riding, and eight solo, cross-country gypsy tours of the United States under her belt. Shortly before her death in 1993, Stringfield said, "I spent most of my life alone, lookin' for a family. I found my family in motorcycling."

LEADERS OF THE PACK

What Dot Robinson and Bessie B. Stringfield accomplished from the 1930s through the 1960s is so profound, it transcends motorcycling.

For starters, Robinson and Stringfield rode their Harleys around the country during an era when the only machinery deemed suitable for women were contraptions built for "women's work"—that is, cooking and scrubbing. Prior to, during, and after World War II, home appliances proliferated like a virus, confining women to indoor labor. While lawn mowers and other gadgets had men toiling *outside* the house, men also had toys that provided an escape. They had motorcycles, cars, even airplanes—machines geared toward freedom, adventure, and leisure. Most women had no such toys that belonged to them alone. The few motorcycle ads that included women usually had them all gussied up, sitting in the sidecar, with condescending text that said things like "Your girl does not have to be an acrobat to get in or out of your sidecar with this new windshield."

And yet, despite this cultural oppression, Dot Robinson and Bessie Stringfield turned motorcycles into their personal freedom machines. And after the war, unlike thousands of Rosie the Riveters, Robinson and Stringfield didn't go back to the kitchen, because they'd never been confined there in the first place.

Robinson was winning endurance contests and she was a partner in a successful, male-dominated business during the decades when women were told not to "steal" jobs from men. While Dot Robinson toured the country alone on two wheels, Betty Friedan (who *later* wrote *The Feminine Mystique* and then became a feminist leader) was taking cooking courses and looking at suburban real-estate ads.[5]

Bessie Stringfield's horizons were so wide, and her career so astounding, during an era when opportunities for most black women were limited to servile roles such as cook, laundress, or maid. What's more, Stringfield broke down color barriers well before Jackie Robinson broke baseball's color barrier in 1947, and well before Rosa Parks ignited the Civil Rights Movement by refusing to give up her seat on an Alabama bus in 1955.

Robinson and Stringfield were two of the boldest and bravest in their day, but they weren't the only women who found freedom, exuberance, and a sense of accomplishment on motorcycles.

In 1938, a woman named Genevieve "Gyp" Baker won the five-hundred-mile Denver Endurance Run in the Colorado Rockies. On New Year's Eve of that year, she rode to the top of Pikes Peak, despite ice and two- and three-foot snowdrifts.[6]

During the Depression, Louise Scherbyn of Waterloo, New York, climbed aboard an Indian Scout; thus began her thirty-year career as a stunt rider and endurance racer. Scherbyn rode her Indian in carnival motordromes, and, in 1940, she performed in what was billed as "America's First All-Girl Motorcycle Show." In 1950, she founded the Women's International Motorcycle Association (WIMA), a correspondence club for riders and passengers.

At around the same time that Scherbyn

Louise Scherbyn on her Indian in 1940.

Vera Griffin Collection

**The Motor Maids at their 1947 convention. On the bikes,
left to right, are Dot Robinson, Vera Griffin, and Helen Kiss Main.**

was getting started in the States, in Wembley, England, a young woman named Theresa Wallach upset her parents by repairing and racing motorcycles. Even though Wallach's mentors included factory designers and racers from British manufacturers like Norton, BSA, and Triumph, male bias shut her out of a local riding club. At school, she hid her activities for fear of being expelled. Yet in 1935, while still a teenager, Wallach and a female roommate decided to take a little trip—*to Africa.* Riding a single-cylinder, 600cc Panther pulling a sidecar and a trailer, they became the first known women to motorcycle across the Sahara Desert alone. Back in England, her riding prowess finally earned her renown. Wallach circled the Brooklands Racetrack on a Norton 350 single, averaging a hundred miles per hour. For this feat, she won the British Motorcycle Club's elite Gold Star award in 1939.

During World War II, she served in the British Army Transport Corps, first as a mechanic, then as a dispatch rider guiding military convoys across a blacked-out England.[7] After the war, Wallach settled in the United States. When novices flocked to the sport on inexpensive Japanese bikes during the seventies, she opened her own teaching facility, the Easy Riding Academy, in Phoenix, Arizona. Wallach summed up her passion for the sport in a 1977 *Road Rider* magazine interview:

> When I first saw a motorcycle, I got a
>
> message from it. It was a feeling—the
>
> kind of thing that makes a person burst

Vera Griffin Collection

Linda Dugeau lead a cow-trailing run with about fifty water crossings through the San Fernando Valley of California.

> into tears hearing a piece of music, or
>
> stand awestruck in front of a painting.
>
> That is what I believe I can teach—that
>
> motorcycling is a tool with which you
>
> can go about accomplishing something
>
> meaningful in your life. It is an art.[8]

Vera Griffin Collection

Nelle Jo Gill in 1945

During the war years and beyond, the AMA's monthly magazine had pages devoted to "Our Girl Riders." The pages were filled with the adventures of the Motor Maids, considered a ladies' auxiliary of the AMA. The Motor Maids and other groups spearheaded social and competitive events to raise funds for the war effort and various charities. There were photos of the club's founder, Linda Dugeau, who was a motorcycle courier in Los Angeles. On weekends, she

Vera Griffin Collection

Helen Kiss Main on her Indian at Daytona Beach, circa 1947.

"cow-trailed"—rode her heavy bike through rock-strewn cow trails in the mountains, forded the iron horse across streams, and made it look easy.

Enthusiast readers were treated to the chronicles of many women, including Nelle Jo Gill, a Motor Maid from Columbus, Indiana. Just months before the bombing of Pearl Harbor in 1941, Gill and her friend Eleanor Stanton rode cross-country on Gill's red and chrome Harley named Lotus Blossom. Their destination was Hollywood; the occasion, a star-studded bowling tournament. The women were decked out in matching black breeches, black satin shirts, and black boots. They must have been a glamorous sight in the eyes of small-town America. During a stop in Salome, Arizona, Gill recalled, "We believe the entire population of 250 came over to our Harley-Davidson and inspected us."[9]

In spite of the pre-wartime tension gripping the nation, Gill and Stanton were free spirits. "It was so simple when we got these unpredictable urges to leave suddenly," wrote Gill in *The Enthusiast*. "Just grab our things, kick over Lotus Blossom and away we'd go— instant transportation—as comfortable and convenient as a magic carpet." Hardly a common sentiment to come from women in those days! The following year, with the United States entrenched in World War II, Gill joined the WAFS. She repaired airplanes, chauffeured generals (including Eisenhower), and was promoted to sergeant.

Another darling of the motorcycle press was Helen Kiss Main of Pottstown, Pennsylvania, the Motor Maids' first treasurer. Her pink

Vera Griffin in 1993.

Indian and matching outfits outdid Dot Robinson's getup, and earned Main the nickname Pink Lady. In 1941, Main won the Typical American Girl Motorcyclist trophy at the Laconia, New Hampshire, rally (the granddaddy of all the big national rallies, dating back to the 1920s). Variations of this award were the National Motorcycle Queen and Most Popular and Typical Girl Rider. Robinson and other Motor Maids were winners, too.

A Motor Maid from Columbus, Indiana, stood out in quiet contrast to Robinson and Main. She was the chubby-cheeked Vera Griffin, who endeared herself to the motorcycle community with her soft-spoken manner and dry humor. Marveling at the pastel outfits worn by her snazzier friends, she once quipped, "In those days, we didn't have blacktop. Dirt roads were sprayed with oil to keep the dust down. Lord knows, I would'a been a mess!"

In 1939, Griffin took a trip with her buddy Ruth as a passenger. "We had cloth helmets, no windshields, and we were filthy," she declared. When they came upon a hill

Vera on her 80-cubic-inch Harley in 1947. That's Louise Scherbyn's Indian in the background.

Vera Griffin Collection

with oil at the crest, she said, "we slid right down, fell off the bike, and it landed on top of us. We were covered in grimy oil." At a rest stop, they rubbed the slime off their skin with gasoline. Griffin chuckled, "The attendant said he didn't see too many women on motorcycles. Then he peered in my face and asked, 'You *are* women, aren't you?' "

In 1940, while working as a toolmaker for an engine company, Griffin and her husband founded the Stoney Lonesome Motorcycle Club. Often she outscored the men at motorcycle field games. She competed in one-thousand-mile, twenty-four-hour marathons and "all-girl reliability trials," in which the women were timed to arrive at checkpoints along a rough course.

In a few short years, Griffin was widowed when her husband lost his life in a trucking accident. She never remarried but maintained a love affair with Harleys, Triumphs, and the road. During a ten-thousand-mile

trip in 1948, when road crews were starting to tame the Wyoming wilderness, Griffin navigated a construction zone laden with live rattlesnakes. Her technique: "I rode with my feet up on the handlebars!" Mind you, the bike was a hardtail—no rear shock absorber—and safety helmets were not yet available.

Over a sixty-year span, Griffin logged more than a million miles throughout the forty-eight contiguous states, Canada, and Mexico. Back home, so beloved was this local matriarch, her cronies named an event for her, Indiana's Own Vera Griffin Meet. Upon her death in 1994 at the age of eighty-one, she was laid to rest in a coffin draped in an orange and black Harley-Davidson banner.

Alice Meyer of Seattle, Washington, in the height of fifties fashion.

From their rolling perches, Griffin and her contemporaries literally rode through time as well as physical space. They putted along the historic Route 66 from Chicago to Los Angeles, once known as "America's Main Street." They rode through a rapidly changing postwar America, whose ideology was reflected in the way that roads and travel changed to accommodate the automobile. As cars became faster and more efficient, winding dirt and gravel back roads gave way to straight, predictable asphalt ribbons. When superhighways tamed the continent, the original meaning of travel—*travail*—was lost on most people. By the 1950s, cars had grown fins and were named for explorers—DeSoto, Hudson, Cadillac—to create the illusion of adventure. As the nation suffocated under Cold War conformity, men controlled the steering wheel, and most women sat passively on the right side of the family sedan.

But not motorcycling women. Like their male peers, they were bored by the idea of driving past the country in a cubicle. Mainstream America hopped in cars for comfort and security, but motorcyclists preferred the risks, the challenges, and the closeness with nature inherent to two-wheeled travel. On a deeper level, for many bikers, the one-on-one experience of riding a motorcycle on an open road was—and still is—a harkening back to archetypal American concepts: freedom, individualism. In this context, the motorcycle is nothing short of a twentieth-century replacement for the horses that pioneers once rode across the frontier. And in the cookie-cutter mentality of the era that produced *Father Knows Best* and *Ozzie and Harriet,* women riders were nothing short of rebels.

Woman on a Harley Hummer

In the early 1960s, even as JFK passed the torch to "a new generation of Americans," and *Feminine Mystique* author Betty Friedan identified "the problem that had no name," hysterical teenagers

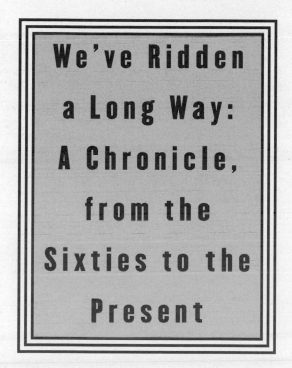

We've Ridden a Long Way: A Chronicle, from the Sixties to the Present

fainted over the Beatles, and girl groups sang about boys, boys, boys. Women's liberation was hardly a mass movement. Media scholar Susan J. Douglas, in *Where the Girls Are: Growing Up Female with the Mass Media,* wondered:

Was I supposed to be an American—individualistic, achievement-oriented, independent? Or was I supposed to be a girl—nurturing, passive, dependent? These warring messages—"be an American; no, no, be a girl"—were amplified and dramatized in the electronic hothouse. . . . We were the first TV generation, [which] gave us psychological mutations all our own.[1]

Beginning in the 1960s, the decade of "free love," advertisements in the motorcycle press changed to reflect loosening sexual mores. Women who had once been buttoned up in sidecars were replaced by girls in bikinis and boots, straddling the backseat or splayed across bikes in Playboy Bunnyesque poses. In the thirties, forties, and fifties, motorcycling had been marketed as a family

OPPOSITE: **Becky Brown, founder of Women in the Wind, on her Harley-Davidson Heritage Softail Classic.**

pastime that husbands could share with their wives; in the sixties and seventies, bikes were (and sometimes still are) marketed to young men as a way to get girls.

Honda's ubiquitous ad campaign, "You Meet the Nicest People on a Honda," did it with a little finesse. Some people believed those ads, with their smiling preppy couples on small, nonthreatening bikes, "redeemed" motorcycling from the headline-grabbing Hell's Angels. But for women riders in those days—women living on the brink of one of the greatest social movements of the twentieth century—it did nothing.

Although it was the era when MEN WORKING signs were replaced with PEOPLE WORKING signs, the media was still leery of strong women. In 1972, during construction of the Eisenhower Memorial Tunnel in the Colorado Rockies, *Life* magazine profiled an engineer and motorcyclist named Janet Bonnema. She was a world traveler and rock climber who rode her only vehicle, a Honda CL350 motorcycle, to work every day. Bonnema was assigned to plot data from instruments in the tunnel, but, unlike the men, she was not allowed *in* the tunnel. Bonnema filed a sex discrimination suit and won. *Life* trivialized her accomplishments by calling her "a rugged superwoman who can bat her eyelashes," adding, "for all her devotion to the cause of women's rights, Janet would rather stay home and make split-pea soup." Even Harley-Davidson's *Enthusiast*, pro-woman for the past sixty years, bowed to prevailing attitudes. In 1976, *The Enthusiast* ran a story about a woman who rode a Harley to her job as a service assistant for Indiana

Bell. The headline blared, NOT LIBERATED— JUST ENJOYING HER MOTORCYCLE.

The now-defunct *Cycle* magazine, looking back at the gender gap, moaned that the "army of New Women" had more passion for their careers than for men. Satirically, *Cycle* said:

Mr. Cheap Tour would welcome women into the sport, if only to keep him company. . . . But, a lot of women hanging around might muss up [guys'] macho image. There is something about a leggy chickster looking fast on a [bike] that sets my blood boiling.[2]

Well, Mr. Cheap Tour be damned, a handful of "leggy chicksters" were already racing. In 1960, Californian Mary McGee was the first woman to compete on a modern asphalt road-racing track. But the few women in cycle sports faced heavy bias. In 1971, dirt track racer Kerry Kleid of Rye, New York, had her license confiscated in the field because "AMA rules did not provide that women could race professionally." A federal district court judge put her back on the dirt track.[3]

On the asphalt, Wendy Epstein of San Francisco recalled: "I was the first woman to gain recognition as a serious racer, but I was also left out of publicity." In 1978, Epstein and Jill Keenan may have been the first all-female team to complete an American Federation of Motorcyclists (AFM) endurance race. Said Epstein: "We raced a 650 Kawasaki for six hours with no pit crew and took second place. We were written up as Keenan and Epstein. No one knew we were women." A year later, Epstein was the fastest privateer (self-supported rider) to qualify for an AMA national superbike race, clocking 163 miles per hour on the straightaway.

"Everyone who beat me was factory sponsored," she said. "As a woman, it was harder for me to get a factory ride." In the early eighties, it was rumored that one company sponsored a slower female rider, probably because the male teammate didn't want to risk being beaten by a woman.

Meanwhile, Tammy Jo Kirk of Dalton, Georgia, was to dirt track racing what Epstein had been to asphalt road racing. Kirk told *Harley Women* magazine: "Most folks don't realize how hard it is for a non-corporate sponsored privateer. We pay our own way, don't always have fresh motors stacked in the van, and often we arrive bone-weary from driving all night to get to the track." Not to mention that privateers do their own wrenching (bike repair and maintenance).

O ut on the highways, women comprised a mere 1 percent of registered motorcycle owners in the 1970s; old-timers say this was a sharp drop from the number of women riding in the thirties and forties, when bikes were a viable alternative to cars.

Beginning in 1969, a street bike that made a splash in the motorcycle press was Honda's four-cylinder CB750. Technologically advanced for its time, the bike was considered a forerunner of today's superbikes. The CB750

ushered in an era where racetrack speeds would be attainable on the nation's new superhighways. For Jhonneen-Lee Finnegan, an African-American and former U.S. Air Force technician with a degree in mechanical technology, the CB750 was an escape from the tightly packed houses that lined her block in Queens, a New York City borough.

Finnegan, then in her twenties, rode her CB750 on a solo, cross-country trip in the early 1970s, when the transcontinental Interstate Route 80 was still under construction. As a young woman enraptured by the speed of the bike, she remembered soaring along I-80 during a pitch-dark night—and suddenly running out of road. Lost in a Midwestern prairie, she said, "I found my way back to civilization by following a flower-painted psychedelic bus filled with friendly hippies."

She recalled: "It was a time when the country had been going through political unrest. I thought, being black, perhaps I should bring a weapon. My mom said, 'If you take it, you might need it; if you don't take it, you won't need it. Just trust in God and everything will be okay.' And it was. People on the road were all so helpful and kind."

Twenty years later, Finnegan attributed that formative journey with shaping the rest of her motorcycling life. Using her technical background, she drew up specifications for state-of-the-art components that turned her six-cylinder Honda GL1500 Gold Wing into a two-wheeled equivalent of a high-performance luxury car. Now working as a psychiatric rehabilitation therapist, Finnegan still enjoys testing her skills by muscling her eight-

Jhonneen-Lee Finnegan with her performance-enhanced 1500cc Honda Gold Wing

hundred-pound "Super Wing" through serpentine roads far from the crowded metropolis.

In 1977, Police Officer Betsy Kreiter made history when she strode across a previously all-male threshold at the Maryland National Capital Park Police Department. Kreiter was the first policewoman in America to become a motorcycle patrol officer. Three years later, Ramona Murray Prieto became the first female motorcycle cop on the California Highway Patrol, where the training regimen was so tough—one cone-weave maneuver was dubbed "The Eliminator"—nearly half of cadets didn't make it.

In another few years, Joanna Needham, a former AMA desert racing champion, broke through the gender barrier in the motorcycle unit of the Los Angeles Police Department. Some days on the job unfolded like the script of a TV cop show. Needham chased criminals on freeways at speeds up to 110 miles per hour and pursued them into twisting canyon roads at night. One time, upon dismounting, she saw her Kawasaki 1000 smashed when a perpetrator floored his car backward and rammed into her bike.

Male reaction to policewomen on wheels was mixed. Needham's colleagues christened her "Puss'n'Boots." Others were treated with suspicion. Recalled Prieto: "When I started riding, people asked me what I was trying to prove, and if I liked girls. 'No!' I said. I just liked riding a motorcycle. I didn't come with any baggage."

In 1978, Debbie Evans, a petite Hollywood stuntwoman, packed her bags for Scotland. At age twenty, Evans rode a motorcycle where few women had ridden before—in the grueling Scottish Six Days observed trials competition.

Observed trials riders must navigate dirt bikes across unforgiving terrain with bike-sucking bogs, sandy hills, boulders, felled trees, and waterfalls. Riders must do wheelies, jump their bikes, change direction in midair, and balance stopped motorcycles without putting a foot to the ground.

Said Evans: "When I got there, people laughed at me because I was a small girl." She rode a 175cc Yamaha, underpowered compared to most of her rivals on 250s and 325s. "People made bets on me in front of my face as to whether I'd last the first day. That just motivated me even more—that made me so mad!"

At the end of the sixth day—after she'd ridden through rain and snow, had her hands frozen to the handlebars and her calves locked in muscle spasms—Evans placed fourth in her class. One observer marveled: "American Debbie Evans put many men to shame. She

In 1988, Officer Kelcy Stefansson became the first woman in the motorcycle patrol of the United States Park Police in Washington, D.C. Astride an 880-pound Harley, she did everything from escort the president's motorcades to the occasional criminal chase.

Lynn Oldenburg

SAFETY AND RIGHTS: "EDUCATE, DON'T LEGISLATE"

"After I started my job as a telephone installer, I realized the importance of the Equal Rights Amendment because there was still harassment. In 1978, I volunteered for the National Organization for Women and helped work on passage of the ERA. We lobbied, passed out flyers, asked people to sign petitions, made phone calls, and wrote letters to legislators. I was a single mother at the time and took my daughter to meetings. . . . I started riding my own motorcycle in the early 1980s and got involved with motorcycle rights because I didn't like anybody telling me what to do. I'm an eighth-generation descendant of Daniel Boone—independence runs strong in my family! I merely transferred my experience with women's rights to activism for motorcyclists."

So said forty-three-year-old Lynn Oldenburg of Highland, Maryland. Oldenburg was one of many women in the seventies and eighties who helped spearhead two grassroots movements that sprung up in the motorcycle community: rider education and safety, and motorcyclists' rights. Oldenburg was both a legislative adviser to American Bikers Aimed Toward Education (ABATE) and a riding instructor for the Motorcycle Safety Foundation (MSF). When the senate threatened to withhold state funds from Maryland's rider education program, Oldenburg and others worked tirelessly to ignite a coalition of motorcyclists who struggled to save the program.

She said, "We took out an ad in the *Washington Post*. We stood in front of the sen-

was the first lady rider in four years and showed remarkable ability in coping with the tough sections. The fact that she can stand on her head in the saddle might help her balance."[4]

Back in Hollywood, the young duchess of hazard went on to a prolific career in stunt work. She successfully rode a motorcycle through explosions and jumped a bike across a sixty-foot ravine. On the other hand, riding through a wall of fire left her with second- and third-degree burns when the flaming wall came with her. A missed landing from a jump off a ninety-four-foot hill left her with a mild concussion. But, said Evans, "I'm not a daredevil, really—I don't ride much on the street."

ate office building with signs that said, 'Save or educate, don't legislate! Save the motorcycle safety program!' We had people going all over the building to see their legislators. They were receptive. It wound up being a compromise bill, but we saved the program."

The motorcyclists' rights movement swelled in the wake of negative media coverage of gangs like the Hell's Angels and the ensuing police crackdowns that occurred in certain pockets of the country. It also occurred in the wake of the rabble-rousing sixties and the civil rights consciousness that pervaded the country.

ABATE, a loosely knit network of statewide organizations, was one of several bikers' rights groups. ABATE originated in the hard-

Wanda Hummel-Schultz

core pages of *Easyriders* magazine and originally stood for A Brotherhood Against Totalitarian Enactments. The group appealed to rough-edged types, including some "outlaw bikers" and anti-establishment crusaders who protested anything that smacked of "Big Brother Government." To this vociferous group, Big Brother was most intrusive when he *ordered* bikers to wear helmets (instead of giving them the choice). The paramount issue —safety—was sometimes lost in all the yelling. Though ABATE changed the meaning behind the acronym and many chapters toned down their act, ABATE as a whole hasn't really shed its hardcore image. Some factions still hold "helmet roasts," a tactic that turns off bikers who believe in wearing helmets.

Beginning in the mid-seventies, an Indiana homemaker named Wanda Hummel-Schultz was, amazingly, able to lead this group. Schultz, a longtime Harley lifestyle biker with a no-nonsense attitude, was the first woman to launch a statewide ABATE organization. Between 1975 and 1982, she became a near-legendary figure and was, in a sense, the personification of ABATE. "I was always telling somebody off while doing good," she chuckled.

Schultz became involved after reading in *Easyriders* "about legislators wanting to put beacons on helmets and seat belts on bikes. I did *not* like it!" She poured herself into a fight to repeal the state's helmet law. "I became a figure," she recalled. "It was seven days a week. There was nothing in my life except ABATE, bikes, riding, and taking care of business. I was always going to meetings, but I had to be home to have supper on the table. My marriage went down the tubes."

Fran Crane made history as an endurance rider but her other passion is sprint racing. Here she is with one of her race bikes.

She added, "I had to work five times harder than a guy to be taken seriously. I sat up all night writing the newsletter, mailed it, and took care of memberships. I was *it* in Indiana. But if I was going to do all the work, I was going to do it my way." They called her the Dictator.

Schultz's legacy was a personal victory. "I did something for *me*," she said. "I was the only woman to start an ABATE organization and make it work. We got the state's helmet law repealed with just 350 members. We proved a point. I made a difference."

Today, the bikers' rights movement fights

A SISTERHOOD IN THE WIND

Becky Brown

"One day in 1979 I was riding my Harley around Toledo and stopped at a light next to a family with a carload of kids. One kid yelled, 'Look, Mom, it's a *girl!*' They'd never *seen* a woman on a motorcycle."

The rider, a twenty-four-year-old factory worker named Becky Brown, had never seen one either, so she placed a tiny newspaper ad seeking other women riders. The initial handful of responses snowballed into a club called Women in the Wind (WITW), which now has six hundred members in twenty American states, four Canadian provinces, and chapters in England and New Zealand.

The members favor Harleys, call one another sisters, and have a sticker that says, "I'm proud to be a lady biker." Their rambunctious humor jumps off the pages of *Shootin' the Breeze,* their newsletter. In one mid-nineties issue, "Reverend Mims" declared, "Being able to conduct weddings, baptisms and funerals is an awesome responsibility. I may not be able to save our souls (or mine). . . . Just one question remains: Do I wear a Dog or a Bitch collar?" Male partners help out at many WITW events.

Today, with so many sisters, Becky Brown can hardly find the time to answer all her mail. She finds herself writing when she'd rather be out riding.

That situation once applied to Californian Arleen Ruby, who founded Women on Wheels (WOW) in 1982. When this club became too large for her to handle, it was shepherded by a string of energetic women. Now, with eighteen hundred members in forty-eight states and five Canadian provinces, WOW is the largest of the all-brand women's clubs. In essence, it is a giant cheerleading squad for motorcycling, with husbands, boyfriends, and fathers doing some cheering, too. Patty Mills of Topeka, Kansas, the club's national director from the late eighties through the early nineties, was the consummate WOW member: mild-mannered and Midwestern . . . yet beneath the genteel exterior was a woman who'd been riding for more than fifteen years throughout North America, Mexico, the United Kingdom, and Europe. Mills, who runs a blueprint business, was elected to the AMA's board of trustees in 1989. Currently, WOW is led by Sue Frish, Susan Konopka, Kathy Heller, and Linda Stone.

Patty Mills

From left, Leenie Bachman, Gin Shear, Sue Slate, and Doris "Book" Buksa are literally on top of the world on the Dempster Highway, Northwest Territory, Canada.

policies that single out or exclude motorcyclists. Besides mandatory helmet laws, activists battle land closures to recreational vehicles, health insurance discrimination, harassment of bikers in groups, and other issues.

WOMEN'S BOOM: THE GREAT 1980S AND '90S

In her classic, *Passages: Predictable Crises of Adult Life*, Gail Sheehy wrote:

Women are much more likely to see a

realm of unimagined opportunities

opening up in the middle years. An

initial sense of danger and timidity may

give way to invigoration. For most of

them, there are still so many firsts ahead.[5]

Indeed, for the many middle-class, thirty-something and over-forty women of the baby-boom generation who got on motorcycles for the first time in the mid-1980s, realms of opportunities did open up—for the independence and self-realization that comes with mastering a motorcycle. What a stroke of luck for bike makers! Professional women with disposable income flexed their muscles and a new market fell into the industry's lap. Sales to women soared.

Foreign motorcycle makers shipped over small cruisers styled to look like Harleys. Honda's 250cc and 450cc Rebels, Yamaha's 250cc Route 66, and Suzuki's 650cc Savage were lighter and much cheaper than Harley's smallest model, the 883cc Hugger. Women bought roughly a third of some entry-level models; with experience, they bought larger bikes. Ads for the smaller imports were targeted to beginners, not women—imagine the droves of men who would've taken up *golf* rather than be seen on "a girl's bike." Harley-Davidson was the only company to court women. Their "I Am Woman, Hear Me Roar" recruitment ads for the club Ladies of Harley became fixtures in some magazines.

By the mid-nineties, industry analysts estimated that seven hundred fifty thousand women were riding motorcycles. Of these, more than five hundred thousand were registered motorcycle owners—a dramatic increase from the seventies. The boom wasn't just fueled by yuppie women. Many working-class readers of *Harley Women* magazine wrote letters on how they scrimped to get on the front seat. Many did so with encouragement from the men in their lives, such as this man, who wrote:

I'm the father of three girls. Raising independent, self-sufficient women was my goal. It takes a special woman to ride a motorcycle, much less THE motorcycle. It takes an independent woman to put up with flack from the lesser females and bros whose own security is a little shakey. Harley Women is an "Atta Girl" affirmation for these unique women.[6]

THE EXISTENTIAL MOTORCYCLIST

One unique woman was Fran Crane, who started riding motorcycles in her teens to rebel against her mother. Crane, now forty-nine, got on a bike, started riding in a straight line, and has hardly put a foot to the ground ever since.

By the late 1980s, this soft-spoken but driven woman had evolved into one of the world's most awesome endurance riders. Crane was an existential motorcyclist, like Jack Kerouac's drivers in *On the Road,* who drove for the sake of pure driving without a destination. Yet for this woman it went deeper. Her numerous marathon riding sessions were self-imposed gauntlets—Crane vs. Crane, Crane vs. machine, Crane vs. the weather and the endless white lines of the interstate.

What was it about Crane that drove her to such literal lengths? She said, "My parents both worked ever since I can remember. I raised my two brothers and cooked meals when I was so small, I had to stand on a chair to reach the stove. Now I don't want any responsibility except for myself."

British émigré Jacqui Sturgess is a founding member of New York City's Sirens, a club with a predominantly lesbian membership. Dating back to 1986, the Sirens are still regarded as one of the nation's leading clubs for gay women, along with Boston's Moving Violations. Sturgess is an advertising executive and just as likely to appear on her bike in a blouse and blazer as in leather. She is terminally ladylike, but turns into a tigress of sorts when defending her turf.

Jacqui Sturgess

Sturgess has helped to give lesbians—whose voices have long been suppressed beneath those of gay men—their proper place. For the Sirens, no other place would do except the very head of New York City's annual gay pride march. "Out Loud, Outrageous, Out Everything!" (an understatement, to say the least) was how one flyer described the event.

With one hundred forty riders in their wake, the Sirens lead the parade. The riders range from prim, feminine corporate types to women with Mohawk haircuts and buttons that scream, "Dyke Bitch from Birth." On that boisterous day, this diverse group of women are united by their pride and their motorcycles.

Crane became the undisputed queen of the elite, long-distance road rally circuit. In 1988, she set a Guinness Book world record for riding her BMW K100 from New York to San Francisco in forty-four hours and twenty minutes. Two years prior, Crane became the first woman to finish in the top ranks of the Iron Butt Rally, riding roughly eleven thousand miles in eleven straight days through horrific levels of sleep denial. She did this two years in a row, placing second and third in a contest so grueling, about half of the entrants drop out.

She said, "You're either too cold, too hot, too tired, too hungry, or a combination of the above to consider the Iron Butt 'fun.' I did it for the challenge. It takes a great deal of physical and mental stamina."

Crane stuck to the helm no matter what. She recalled, "One night on the way to Jacksonville, Florida, I rode into the worst storm I'd ever been in. The water was so high on the pavement, it knocked my feet off the footpegs. I couldn't pull off because I couldn't see. Then lightning struck in front of me. It came so close I thought I'd been hit and had died. I touched myself to see if I was alive."

Crane started motorcycle sprint racing—six to eight laps on a high-speed track—with the same intensity. While working as a parking enforcement officer in Santa Cruz, California, she moonlighted to pay off debts racked up from her passion. Crane has lived with her boyfriend for twenty years but they are not married. She said, "Walter knows this is what I want to do and he will not stop me. That's one reason we're still together."

FANTASTIC VOYAGERS

While Crane was testing her endurance on the rally circuit, New Yorker Tabitha Estabrook, a recent graduate of Amherst College, tested her endurance in what some say was the ultimate motorcycle ride: a twenty-month voyage around the world. Her companions were her then-boyfriend, Jim Rogers, a self-made Wall Street millionaire, and a stream of motorcyclists from different countries who shared the journey with them.

Estabrook was twenty-four and fresh out of the MSF beginning rider course. She learned to tear down and rebuild their BMW twins, said good-bye to her family, and in March 1990 set off on a journey that was as profoundly internal as it was outward and physical. For every one of the 57,354 miles she rode, challenges were flung her way. In between the exotic cultures and spectacular sights, Estabrook dealt with broken roads, broken bikes, bad weather, bureaucratic bumblings, illness, relationship rifts, and self-doubt.

"For the first six months, I was wretched," she admitted. "Early in the trip on horrible Yugoslavian roads, Jim was leading, pressing to make time, trying to get me to pass with him. I was a novice on a 1967 600cc bike. He was an experienced rider on a 1989 1000cc bike. There was oncoming traffic and I couldn't complete the pass. I put on too much rear brake and the motorcycle fishtailed. I lost control, the bike flew into a ditch, and I slid hard on the pavement. Fortunately, I had my

helmet and full leathers on, so I really didn't get hurt."

In Siberia, she said, "we rode our heavy street bikes over roads that were piled with grapefruit-sized rocks or mired in mud. There, Jim fell and his bike broke down. I was the mechanic, so now I was an asset and an old dynamic between us changed. My confidence, and thus my abilities, went up." In a remote Siberian village, Estabrook helped hand-machine steel parts from a truck engine, to replace the parts on Rogers's bike that had failed.

From there, she rode through everything from the shifting sands of the Sahara Desert to monstrous thunderstorms in the Australian outback before returning to Manhattan in November 1991.

"People tell me how brave I was," she said. "I was just stubborn. This trip was about stretching myself beyond what I was and trying on something new. Up till then, it was the most important thing I'd done. But at age thirty, I hope it's not the greatest thing. Children will be just as great."

In July 1993, four weary, mud-caked women rode into the village of Inuvik in the Arctic Circle. It was one-thirty in the morning. Under the glare of a twenty-four-hour sun, the women dismounted from three weather-beaten BMWs and a patched-up Yamaha. After riding 4,500 miles across the top of the United States and into Canada, they had just conquered the Dempster Highway—all 480 rutted, gravelly, kidney-jarring miles of it. The women hugged and jumped up and down triumphantly. They

Gloria "Gee Gee" Green

had just reached a frontier that few humans ever see: the northernmost town accessible by land on the continent.

The lead riders were Gin Shear, a forty-three-year-old computer programmer, and Sue Slate, forty-six, a remedial-reading teacher. These women had been riding together and sharing a household in upstate New York since the mid-1970s. With them were their friends, Bostonian Leenie Bachman and Canadian Doris Buksa.

On their bug-splattered, gravel-scratched windshields were decals that read, "Women Riding for Research, Arctic Tour '93." Slate and Shear had publicized the ride through the Women's Motorcyclist Foundation, their not-for-profit networking group. In so doing, they

inspired thousands of North Americans to contribute more than thirty thousand dollars to the Susan G. Komen Breast Cancer Foundation. Said Slate, "No matter how many hardships we dealt with on this journey, there was nothing we did that could compare to the courage of a person fighting breast cancer."

Empowered by their achievement, Slate and Shear launched another campaign—Pony Express Tour '96, National Ride for Breast Cancer Research. The plan called for at least ninety teams of women to gather donations, then ride legs around the nation's perimeter. In the spirit of the old Pony Express, at the end of every leg, the lead "cowgirl" would pass to the next leader a medallion and scroll containing the names of people affected by the disease.

With grace and determination, and by blending with the sport's various factions, Slate and Shear have done what few in society have done. They have rallied a broad spectrum of people—straight, gay, female, and male—behind a common cause, the fight against breast cancer.

WE'VE RIDDEN A LONG WAY

"There's nothing women can't do. We can even stand up and pee." This was the attitude that put African-American Gloria "Gee Gee" Green at the head of the Five-Borough Motorcycle Association, a male-dominated coalition of black and Latino clubs in New York City and Long Island. Green, fifty-one, has six foster children and works with mentally disabled youngsters. Clubs in her coalition do charity work and deliver toys to children's hospitals.

Across the nation, there are more than half a million women of varied backgrounds who are like Gloria Green. They are united by a bond, a love of two-wheeled travel. As Green exuberantly demonstrates, women represent the full spectrum of motorcycling—as a passion, a lifestyle, a sport, a platform to advance larger causes, and a statement of personal independence. As motorcycling has grown into a facet of American life with its own subcultures, folklore, and history, in every way, women, just like men, have played an integral role in its evolution. And for many women, motorcycling has played an integral role in their lives, often becoming inseparable from their self-image. A rider named Billye Nipper, in a recent issue of *Women on Wheels* magazine, put it like this:

> *I have an identity crisis. I am a professional contracting officer for the federal government. I hold a master's degree in Criminal Justice Administration. I have a husband, a house and a garden. I sell cosmetics part-time and I ride a motorcycle! I am proud of me. I have tried many things, such as downhill skiing, golf and distance running, but nothing has challenged me more or has been more exciting than riding a motorcycle. . . . I learned you get instant respect when you're wearing a black leather jacket and riding boots. When you go to the Dairy Queen in Tishomingo, Oklahoma, on Sunday after church, people stare at you and are fascinated. Kids in passing vehicles point you out to their parents. You are something out of the norm. You are defying society's rules. You are a woman on a motorcycle.[7]*

WILD AT HEART

Marlon Brando meets Madonna as black leather combines with fishnet, rap jewelry, pearls, and soft skirts for a sexy new look

"That's the woman who wears my jeans— she's independent, she's hot, and she knows how to ride that Harley-Davidson."

—Calvin Klein on *20/20*, referring to biker-model Carré Otis

"Yo! Put your collars on! You're the Sluts! Try 'n' act like it!"

—Dialogue from *Chopper Chicks in Zombietown*, a 1991 B movie about an all-girl motorcycle gang

"I'm a mom, a wife, and a crazy performer who likes to drive a motorcycle and kick up her heels."

—Ann-Margret, writing in her 1994 autobiography[1]

"Straight chicks, take notes! I'm property. I'm possessed. I'm a biker's ol' lady."

—Anonymous, *Outlaw Biker* magazine, 1990

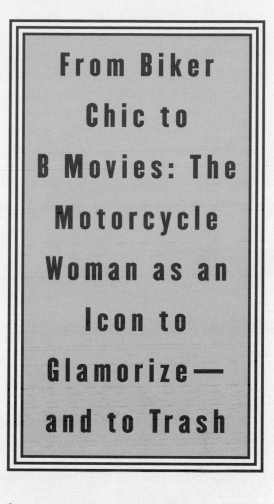

From Biker Chic to B Movies: The Motorcycle Woman as an Icon to Glamorize— and to Trash

Beginning in the early to mid-1990s, as part of a pop culture phenomenon dubbed "biker chic," women on motorcycles pervaded the media. Motorcycling women became icons for trend watchers and trendsetters to glamorize—and to trash. Everyone from Geraldo Rivera to *Vogue* editor Anna Wintour had something to say about motorcycling women, or, more precisely, something to

OPPOSITE: *Vogue*'s version of biker chic. The idea was to conjure up the gang scenes of *The Wild One*. Not an easy task with those skirts.
(Peter Lindbergh/Originally appeared in *Vogue*, Sept. 1991)

gain from exploiting real and imagined women on bikes.

Fashion designers, women's magazines, "trash TV" hosts, B movie directors, sitcom writers, music video producers, comic book artists, celebrities in the worlds of entertainment, sports, and politics, and advertisers of a range of goods—from perfume and jeans to hair- and nail-care products—have cast the motorcycling woman as a creature with multiple personalities. As the opening quotes suggest, the media's portrayal of motorcycling women has been nothing short of schizoid.

Depending on the eye of the beholder (or, rather, the media purveyor), a woman on a motorcycle must be a vampiress on wheels, as in DC Comics' *Vamps;* a swaggering broad, as

in the B flick *Chopper Chicks in Zombietown;* or a jiggle-TV bimbo, as in an episode of *Married with Children,* in which teen tramp Kelly crashes a bike.

If a motorcycling woman is gay—some lesbians are just as good at reinforcing "dykes on bikes" stereotypes—then she must be an Amazon, as in "Hog Heaven,"[2] an erotic short story in which the sex object is a bull dyke named Sam. Just Sam, thank you, ma'am. On the other hand, the motorcycling woman may even turn up as the latest incarnation of that perpetually heterosexual, but eternally frustrated, Cosmo Girl. In 1994, *Cosmopolitan* magazine gave us a photo of a stunning, leather-clad woman astride a Harley, raising her arms in a V-for-victory

LLOYD KAUFMAN AND MICHAEL HERZ PRESENT A TROMA TEAM RELEASE
CHOPPER CHICKS IN ZOMBIETOWN
"JOE BOB SAYS CHECK IT OUT" —JOE BOB BRIGGS, Dallas Observer
MOVIES OF THE FUTURE TROMA INC.

Courtesy Troma, Inc.

In *Vamps,* "Whipsnake" hunts for "men who would be meals."

salute. The photo illustrated an article titled "You Can Be Single and Live a Rich, *Full* Life." Obviously, this Cosmo Girl no longer needs a husband—and who needs that teeny vibrator when she can straddle a Big Twin?

The message purveyed by each of these images is that it's not quite normal for a woman to ride a motorcycle. That is, unless she's a star, a model, or a "rubbie," a rich urban biker. Then—about-face!—she's chic.

In the early nineties, it became fashionable to be a rebel, or at least look the part. The year 1989 had seen the launch of Harley-

Davidson MotorClothes, with motorcycle fashions that were functional and attractive. Soon after, the alluring mix of women, motorcycles, and leather exploded from the runways of Paris and New York to chic magazines like *Vogue* and *Harper's Bazaar,* and to retail stores from Saks Fifth Avenue to Sears.

Calvin Klein was among the first designers outside the motorcycle industry to note that female riders had the look that many non-riding women would imitate. In October 1991, Klein published an unprecedented, 116-page fashion ad supplement to *Vanity Fair*

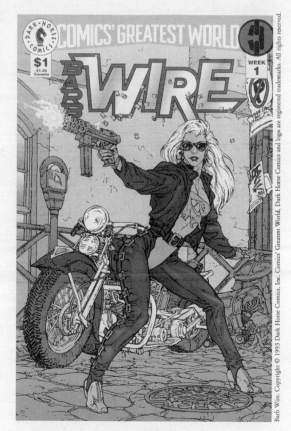

Pamela Lee of TV's *Baywatch* stars as the motorcycling "superbabe" in the film version of *Barb Wire.*

Courtesy Harley-Davidson MotorClothes

Harley-Davidson MotorClothes set the standard for biker chic.

mechanic named Ross Langlitz. He designed it strictly for function, yet four decades after Marlon Brando wore it in 1954's *The Wild One,* the biker jacket and what it symbolizes —rebellion—had been vaulted to the status of an American classic.

The fixation with biker fashions ranged from the all-too-serious to the ridiculous. *Vogue* published a dreamy photo essay with models in motorcycle jackets over taffeta dresses and hip-hop jewelry. The models posed with Triumphs and Harleys, similar to the bikes in *The Wild One.* A couple of the portraits were included in *On the Edge: Images from 100 Years of Vogue* (Random House, 1992), a milestone hardcover anthology and

magazine; its theme was a woman, tattooed biker-model Carré Otis, on a motorcycle. During a *20/20* television interview, Klein told Barbara Walters: "*That's* the woman who wears my jeans—she's independent, she's hot, and she knows how to ride that Harley-Davidson."

Chanel, Donna Karan, Anne Klein, and other top designers usurped the biker look, prompting *Vogue* to sniff: "Redesigning the ubiquitous motorcycle jacket seems to be the fashion challenge of the nineties." Indeed, the street—actually, the road—had come to couture. The black leather biker jacket, with its asymmetrical zipper, wind flap, epaulets, belt, and longer waistline in back, was reputedly invented in the early forties by a Harley

Patrice Stable/Courtesy Thierry Mugler

Thierry Mugler's motorcycle bustier

museum exhibit. The nation's foremost purveyor of chic had elevated to landmark status
images of women bikers who were feminine
to the nth degree.

Subscribing to the theory that fashions are
a reflection of a culture, even *The New York
Times* pontificated: "Women have long borrowed key phrases from the fashion vocabu-
lary of men. The process seems to involve
some kind of appropriation of the symbols of
independence, toughness and power ... the
motorcycle look allows women to be tough
and feminine at the same time."[3]

It also allowed them to spend saddlebags of
money. In 1992, Harley-Davidson Motor-
Clothes reportedly raked in about $49 mil-

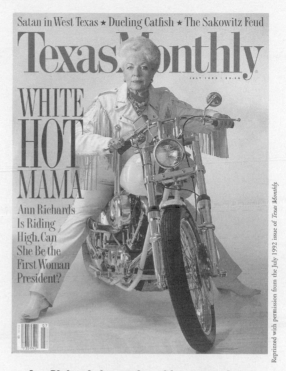

Ann Richards learned to ride at age sixty.

Malcolm Forbes, Elizabeth Taylor, and
"Passion," the Sportster he gave her in 1987.

lion, much of it from urbanites who didn't
ride.[4] Harley put its bar and shield logo on
practically everything, even a swimwear line
with studded bikinis! Biker chic went truly
berserk when French designer Thierry Mugler
built a metal and Plexiglas bustier with a headlight, handlebars, and rearview mirrors. Then,
all those *Vogue* models who couldn't actually
ride a motorcycle could at least wear one.

At the same time, it was an era when feminist themes had pervaded advertising. The
motorcycling woman was a logical icon of the
times: She was independent and free—a
modern-day Annie Oakley on wheels. In a
prime-time commercial for Lady Stetson perfume, a cowgirl astride a motorcycle roared off
into the sunset—with her cowboy on the *back*

Lance Stadler/Botaish Group

k.d. lang on her Harley Springer

seat. Revlon even put Cindy Crawford on the front seat of a cycle to sell hair conditioner.

Clinging to the coattails of chic, a gaggle of VIP wanna-be bikers began using, and continue to use, motorcycles and bikerwear to boost their image as sex symbols, rebels, or powerful dudettes. A leather-clad Elizabeth Taylor, celebrating her sixtieth birthday in the February 1992 issue of *Life,* proved she was one sexy sexagenarian. Taylor lounged on Passion, the purple Sportster given to her by Malcolm Forbes, the late billionaire biker and patron saint of rubbies.

Six months later, when political hypesters had former Texas governor Ann Richards poised for national office, Richards appeared on the cover of *Texas Monthly.* A commanding figure in white fringed leather, she straddled a Harley next to the headline WHITE HOT MAMA: ANN RICHARDS IS RIDING HIGH. CAN SHE BE THE FIRST WOMAN PRESIDENT? Well, no. But as a sixtieth birthday present to herself, Richards did learn to ride that bike.

Then, genuine longtime motorcyclists who happened to be celebrities posed on their bikes for paparazzi. Wynonna Judd, who rode while touring, told *People* magazine: "The Harley gives me a chance to pull up beside fans just long enough for them to recognize me, and then I pull away. If you lose the child within yourself, you might as well give up."

k. d. lang, riding motorcycles since childhood, told *Vanity Fair:* "I love the feel of them. I love the wind. I love the aloneness. I like the romance of being on a motorcycle."

Ann-Margret, who has ridden Triumphs and Harleys for about thirty years, has often used bikes during her kitschy Las Vegas stage shows. In her autobiography, she wrote: "People who saw [me as] the performer astride a motorcycle on stage, hair wild, body contorting, could not have envisioned the shy woman inside. By now I had reconciled myself to the two Ann-Margrets."[5]

HOW HARLEY'S MYSTIQUE BEGAT BIKER CHIC

Why all the hoopla over motorcycles and bikers? Much symbolism is attached to the motorcycle. It is an emotionally charged object. Many bikers view the motorcycle as an extension of their personality, a way to stand out, make a statement, and, in some cases, it is a vehicle by which they have reinvented themselves.

Clyde Earl Collection

Ann-Margret years ago on her Triumph T100. In her autobiography, A-M said she wasn't heavy enough to easily kickstart her bikes. Amused fellow actors once strapped a lead belt to her waist. It helped.

"On stage, I talk to my audiences about my love of riding," says country singer Tanya Tucker. "I tell them I have a hot pink Harley. Then I go into a song about independence." Tucker, now thirty-seven, started riding at age nine on a Honda 150.

The motorcycle—specifically, the Harley-Davidson motorcycle—has been elevated to the status of an American pop culture icon. Harleys are right up there with Elvis, rock 'n' roll, and baseball. When an object attains that hallowed status, enter the trend watchers and exploitation artists. They take what is timeless and classic in American life, stylize it to make it seem exclusive, and then sell it back to the masses. That was the essence of "biker chic," which was an aberration of its predecessor, the Harley-Davidson "mystique."

The Harley-Davidson mystique is a nebu-lous concept that has riveted the media for decades and taken root in the hearts and minds of Harley lovers around this entire planet.

The word *mystique* has been defined by Webster's as "a complex of transcendental or somewhat mystical beliefs and attitudes developing around an object." The Harley mystique as we know it today combines patri-otism, rebel-heroism, and Yankee ingenuity with Hollywood schmaltz and commercial-ism. It's very American.

The *seed* of the mystique lies in the fact that the Harley-Davidson Motor Company,

Gene Tierney, 1940s bombshell, was said to have tooled around Hollywood on a Harley.

aerodynamic plastic, chrome-laden Harleys are built to cruise boulevards, to be admired as the rolling pieces of artwork that they are.

And yet there were times when Harley struggled to survive, especially in the 1970s. The Japanese had flooded the market with cheap, reliable bikes, while Harley, then owned by AMF (a bowling ball maker), churned out leaky, persnickety dinosaurs. This, along with economic and other factors, nearly shut the Motor Company down. Senior management employees saved the day when, in 1981, they bought it from AMF.

In 1983, Harley engineers unveiled the Evolution engine, a revamped version of the

founded in Milwaukee, Wisconsin, in 1903, is the only American motorcycle maker remaining from a field that once had 150 domestic competitors. (Indian, the penultimate survivor, ceased production in 1953.) The *soul* of the mystique is Harley's primitive, pushrod V-twin engine. It may be technologically outdated, yet its deep, rumbling vibration, and the thundering roar of the pipes, can make any person astride Milwaukee iron feel larger than life. Harleys, or "hogs," as they are nicknamed, are also distinctive for their nostalgic, "retro" look—some models closely resemble Harleys of the fifties. Unlike streamlined foreign bikes that are covered in

Motor Maid Bernice Miles tooled around Peoria, Illinois, on the same bike as Tierney's.

A parade of 68,000 motorcycles shook
the highway to celebrate Harley's
ninetieth anniversary.

pushrod V-twin, along with other improve-
ments. Just as important, Harley's marketeers
gave the mystique a face-lift. In the era of
Ronald Reagan and the newly minted "yuppies," Harley courted this new, upscale bunch
by forming the Harley Owners Group
(HOG). By providing a family-oriented network of clubs, riders had a new weekend pastime, instant camaraderie, and a reason to
stick with the product. The company was also
the first motorcycle maker to recognize the
sea changes occurring among women. They
courted *this* new market with Ladies of
Harley, an offshoot of HOG. With the introduction of the Hugger, an 883cc Sportster
with a twenty-seven-inch seat height, Harleys
became accessible to even the most inseam-
challenged women. By 1994, women bought

twenty-four percent of all Sportsters. Times
had certainly changed; in the old days, one
popular magazine called the Sportster "the
man's machine of men's machines."

In 1993, the Motor Company celebrated its
ninetieth anniversary with much media
fanfare. A Harley ad declared: "We've survived four wars, a depression, a few reces-
sions, 16 U.S. presidents, foreign and
domestic competition . . . and one Marlon
Brando movie." That movie, *The Wild One,*
became an unlikely cornerstone of the mystique and forever changed the public's percep-
tion of motorcyclists. Brando played the
leader of a cycle gang that terrorized a town.
The film, released in the mid-fifties, was
based on an actual incident that occurred in
1947 in Hollister, California. The rumble
made the cover of *Life* magazine; on the coffee tables of America sat a drunken biker on a
stripped-down Harley amid a pile of beer
cans. A horrified public gaped at a new breed
of youth gangs, "outlaw bikers," whom *Wild
One* director Stanley Kramer called "the first
big divorcement of youth from society."

Although Brando rode a British Triumph in
The Wild One, the movie had enough bad guys
on Harleys to cement the image of the Harley
rider as a hoodlum. Harley was stuck with the
outlaw image, which Hollywood perpetuated
in dozens of bad-biker flicks that invaded drive-
ins, mainly throughout the 1960s and '70s.

Meanwhile, a small but real outlaw biker
subculture had spread from its California
roots. The Harley-loving Hell's Angels, formed
in the late 1940s by rowdy, ex–World War II
airmen, were fascinating fodder for countless

reporters and scholars. The most sensational account of the Angels' raw, tribal subculture was Hunter Thompson's 1967 best-seller, *Hell's Angels: A Strange and Terrible Saga.*

The legendary Angels begat other gangs or "clubs" of dubious distinction. Like Kerouac's beat generation, or the rebel-hero personified by James Dean, the first outlaw bikers sprung from disillusionment with the nation's conformist society during the Cold War era. But a few clubs evolved beyond youthful rebellion to become organized criminal entities.

The dominant players in outlaw tribes have always been men who are, for the most part, misogynists. Their women have been relegated to backseat status in every respect. Some outlaw women have been victims of the subculture's more sordid aspects, but others have been willing participants. Some outlaw women were runaways from abusive families; gang life was preferable to the conditions that had driven them from home.[6]

Among these women, from the earliest days there had been social strata. An outlaw biker's "old lady" was his wife or significant other. On her vest, she sometimes wore a patch indicating she was the "property of" her man. The sorry person at the bottom of this society was the outlaw biker "mama," who was the sexual property of the whole gang. Labels such as "biker chick" and "biker babe" loosely referred to outlaw women but did not confer any rank.

The American Motorcyclist Association had a public-relations nightmare on its hands. An AMA spokesman declared that outlaws comprised a mere 1 percent of all motorcyclists. The statement backfired when outlaws defiantly adopted the label. Adding a "1%er" patch to their vests, they perpetuated their own myth.

In 1969, hippies hit the road in *Easy Rider.* The Harley-riding drifters portrayed by Peter Fonda and Dennis Hopper nearly sanctified outlaws and enshrined yet another facet of the mystique—the lone, latter-day "cowboy"—in contemporary American folklore. The motorcycle had reached near-mythical proportions, or at least that is what the entertainment industry, and not necessarily motorcycle makers, had the public believing.

Meanwhile, Harley franchises were reluctant to service the more unshaven, beer-bellied, and tattooed devotees of the marque, so outlaws turned to chop shops. There, backyard mechanics spawned the cult of Harley customizing. The steed of the latter-day cowboy was not a stock Harley, but a "chopper," a lean, stripped-down machine. The hallmarks of choppers were their radically extended front forks, high handlebars, and low, laid-back seats.

Before long, the custom cult spread beyond the outlaw community, and the minimalist ethic gave way to the American penchant for chrome. The business of customizing Harleys (and other bikes) blossomed into a full-fledged aftermarket industry chock-full of specialty parts. Custom Harleys became personalized statements. Hand-painted murals and flame motifs graced gas tanks and fenders, chromed parts gleamed, and exhaust pipes turned into fishtails and bell tips. The custom cult grew into a flamboyant, worldwide phenomenon and nowadays, the price of entry ain't cheap—people who can afford biker chic fashions may spend thirty thousand dollars to create a boutique bike. Nearly three-fourths of today's Harley owners are college-educated, and their

KITTEN ON WHEELS WITH HER BIKE... HER BOOTS and BIKINI

Out for kicks...in for trouble! She's going to Join the...

BORN LOSERS

FROM *AMERICAN INTERNATIONAL* IN **COLOR**

RECOMMENDED FOR MATURE AUDIENCES

median income has shot up to forty-three thousand dollars. Designer-store dealerships now hang MotorClothes next to the motor oil.

HOG and Ladies of Harley, still going strong with two hundred eighty thousand members, continue to offer riders a pleasant alternative to "hardcore" biker gatherings, where the clientele can be pretty rough. At HOG rallies, doctors, lawyers, and executives mingle comfortably with working-class "lifestyle bikers." Bearded men in black T-shirts and women in leather boots, vests, and chaps are the hallmarks of the "lifestyle." Since yuppies have adopted these costumes, bank presidents are indistinguishable from bartenders. The mystique has been gentrified—the toupeed and the toothless are now equally chic.

CYCLE SLUTS AND BITCHES: HOW WOMEN ARE PORTRAYED IN B BIKER FLICKS

Far, far from the rubbie rallies and the fashionable pages of *Vogue* are the girl gangs in the B biker flicks. And when you look at how women have been portrayed in these films, you have to wonder how biker chic could have sprung from the same leather-jacketed seed.

"Remember this, Mama! We ain't no bunch of daisy-pullin' broads. We are the Maneaters, and we live up to the rules or we pay! Now get on that cycle and ride!"

So seethed Queen, the raven-haired, chain-wielding lead villainess of *She-Devils on Wheels.* This B movie had the Maneaters, a vicious, bisexual girl gang, drag-racing for "meat" (sex with wimpy, captive guys). But when one girl developed a crush on her wimp, Queen forced her to tie him to her rear fender and drag him across the asphalt. The

gang's motto: "Sex, guts, blood, and all men are mothers!" That was back in 1968, reflecting, perhaps, the angrier side of the women's movement and a crude attempt at revenge for film violence against women.

"I know I'm a bitch, but, fuckin' A, I gotta be to keep these little pussies together."

So barked Rox, the raven-haired, bullwhip-wielding, lesbian leader of the pack in *Chopper Chicks in Zombietown.* This *1991* B flick had the Cycle Sluts, a girl gang of misfits, stopping in sleepy towns for "meat" (sex with any available penis or penile surrogate). Not much had changed in a couple of decades. Dede was the straight chick who punched her husband and sighed, "Homes and husbands and families are for normal people. I just don't hack it as normal."

Hellcats, Angels Wild Women, Hell's Belles, The Miniskirt Mob, and *Bury Me an Angel* were among the slew of B biker movies of the sixties and seventies. In these and other films, women were almost exclusively portrayed in the context of the outlaw strata. They were generally depicted as domineering shrews, social outcasts, drug-crazed hippies, whores, lesbian bull dykes, or cloying, submissive pieces of property who were verbally abused, slapped, or raped. In most cases, they were shown riding on the backseat.

In the few films where women had the upper hand, or when they rode their own bikes, they were sociopathic man-haters wielding whips, guns, knives, and chains (much like the men). In the final scene of the awful *She-Devils,* they decapitated a man. The women in the bizarre *Easy Wheels,* a throwback released in 1986, were radicals who

MEET THE
DEBUTANTE IN A
LEATHER SKIRT

Too Young...Too Tough
...Too itching for Action
to Look for it--
She'll make it
Where she is!

"HELL'S BELLES"
...COLOR by BERKEY-PATHÉ

M Suggested for MATURE audiences
(parental discretion advised)

STARRING
JEREMY SLATE · ADAM ROARKE · JOCELYN LANE
WRITTEN BY JAMES GORDON WHITE AND R. G. McMULLEN · PRODUCED & DIRECTED BY MAURY DEXTER
A MAURY DEXTER PRODUCTION · AN AMERICAN INTERNATIONAL PICTURE
©1969 American International Pictures

EXPLOITATION

SET IT ON YOUR STAGE OR IN YOUR LOBBY

LOCAL WEDDING
MOTOR-FASHION SHOW

Artwork copyright © Orion Pictures Corporation

Film companies gave promotional material like this to movie houses to exploit the sexy "biker babes" in B movies of the 1960s and '70s.

hated everything in the universe—they stole girl babies to be raised by wolves. In the rare cases where female characters had brains or integrity, they were punished. In 1967's *Born Losers,* a college student who had the audacity to ride her own bike was beaten and raped by a male cycle gang. In *Stone Cold,* another throwback released in 1991, the sole biker chick with a speaking part had a moral conscience; for that, she was shot in the head.

And yet while female characters were frequently raped (usually off-camera), the films rarely delivered the sex touted in the ludicrous publicity copy. The lobby poster for 1971's *Angels Hard as They Come* promised "Big Men with Throbbing Machines and the Girls Who Take Them On!" The one for *Bury Me an Angel* blared about "A howling hellcat humping a hot steel hog on a roaring rampage of revenge." Ads for 1969's *Hell's Belles* leered "Meet the debutante in a leather skirt. Too young, too tough, too itching for action to look for it—she'll make it where she is!"

Rarely in the movies have there been portrayals of heroines or even just regular women (or men) on motorcycles. While 1985's *Mask* had Cher glamorizing the life of Rusty Dennis, a true-life 1%er woman, she was

UPGRADING THE IMAGE

Beyond motorcycling, there are few other pastimes, few other lifestyles, that have been exploited so relentlessly by B movie makers. And there are few other pastimes, few other lifestyles, that are as controversial among *non*participants. This is why the majority of honest, law-abiding motorcyclists are obsessed with projecting a positive image. What the nonriding public thinks has real safety ramifications to every rider in traffic.

What the biker chic phenomenon did for motorcyclists was foster a media blip of positive coverage. Human-interest articles appeared with titles like "Boomer Bikers," "Heck's Angels," and "The Mild Ones." The names of Malcolm Forbes and others in his riding club, the Capitalist Tools, were bandied about. Harley-Davidson gave a New York entrepreneur permission to use its logo and re-creations of its V-twin engine to decorate the Harley-Davidson Cafe, a theme restaurant where tourists can pose on a bike in front of a "Harleywood" sign. Visa filmed a TV commerical at Cleveland's Southeast Harley-Davidson dealership, which the owners had turned into a mini-mall with a diner and a kiddie carousel. Yet biker chic had little impact for women riders beyond expanding their wardrobe choices—though not by much, as butter-soft pastel leather doesn't cut it for serious riding.

Mary Hart, cohost of TV's *Entertainment Tonight,* is a regular at the annual Love Ride in Glendale, California. The event, which benefits the Muscular Dystrophy Association, brings out Hollywood's celebrity motorcyclists.

shown as a chemically dependent victim, not really a heroine, nor did she ride her own bike. Perhaps the only *Thelma and Louise*–type biker heroines appeared in two recent, obscure TV movies. *Shame* was a remake of an Australian film about a motorcycling lawyer who helped rape victims. In *The Stranger,* a foxy vigilante turned out to be a ghost who violently avenged her own rape and murder. In both films, the heroines were icy and unsympathetic.

For forty years, actually, the American Motorcyclist Association had been trying to downplay the fallout from *The Wild One* and the few real biker gangs whose doings became fodder for movies like *Wild Angels*

Courtesy Hardly Angels

VIPs who are genuine bikers have joined the "positive image" campaign. Linda Nighthorse Campbell (seated, second from left), a math teacher and wife of U.S. senator Ben Nighthorse Campbell, helped form what may be the first all-women motorcycle drill team in 1995. Called Hardly Angels, the team is "a chorus line on cruisers" that does figure-eights, V-formations, and other precision maneuvers. Lynell Corbett (standing, far right), a real-estate manager and former dance instructor, choreographs the drills. The women are mostly in their forties and fifties and are based in Durango, Colorado. Says Campbell, "At parades, people's reactions to us are amazing. First they see the bikes coming. Then they realize we're all women and they just go crazy."

Jo Giovannoni of *Harley Women*

In 1994, innocent motorcyclists at a Red Cross benefit ride in South Carolina were allegedly harassed, searched, and videotaped by police. This bizarre incident prompted the American Civil Liberties Union to file a class-action civil rights lawsuit against the South Carolina authorities. All this, in spite of biker chic.

In the 1980s, "Discover Today's Motorcycling" (DTM), a public-relations effort of the trade's Motorcycle Industry Council, found that 89 percent of media coverage of real motorcyclists was negative. DTM and the AMA knew that women could "soften" the sport's image. In 1987, four yuppie women were given new bikes to ride across the country, a gimmick to commemorate the 1916 transcontinental ride of Adeline and Augusta Van Buren. The media bit, including *The New York Times*, which marveled, "Yes, Real Women Do Ride Motorcycles."

and *Satan's Sadists.* As a result of these negative imprints, even today, it is not uncommon for law-abiding riders, male and female, on any brand of bike, and no matter how well dressed, to be targets of misplaced hostility. A misinformed public thinks that anyone who rides a motorcycle must be out for trouble. Motorcyclists have been deliberately run off the road by car and truck drivers. Bikers have faced discrimination in housing and have been prohibited from bringing their vehicles into recreational areas where cars are allowed.

Jo Giovannoni, a lifestyle biker from a Chicago suburb, took a different, more homespun approach. With her friend Chris Sommer, Giovannoni cofounded *Harley Women* magazine as a clean, family-oriented alternative to the biker skin rags that catered to the hardcore crowd. Many *Harley Women* articles are straight-from-the-heart readers' letters. They consider themselves independent, but since husbands and boyfriends read the magazine also, they choose words carefully to avoid treading on the egos of "the menfolk." Until recently, the *other* F word— feminism—was almost as taboo as owning a "rice burner" (Japanese bike). This prompted a reader nicknamed T-Bone to react:

You seem anxious to show you do not endorse women's lib. It's true there are militant types in all groups who give it a bad name. True feminists don't want to be like men, they just want to be free to be the best women they can be. If that means being a wife and mother, or an engineer, cop or waitress, or riding motorcycles, it isn't important. . . . Please don't put feminism in the category of militant women. None of us would like it much if we were told we couldn't ride because of our sex!

To which Giovannoni replied, "Guess we are true feminists after all. We just don't feel we have to prove anything to anyone about the fact that we like to ride motorcycles. Right, ladies?"

WOMEN IN THE DUAL-AUDIENCE MOTORCYCLE PRESS

As for the sophisticated, slick motorcycle magazines targeted to sport and touring riders of (mainly imported) bikes: You'd think they would be a safe haven for serious women riders. Think again. A small but growing percentage of articles are written by women. And a handful of female editors appear on the mastheads of fine magazines. Yet *advertisers,* especially in the sport magazines geared to the young, male, raging-hormone crowd, still use women's bodies to sell bikes and accessories. With the exception of a few periodicals, ads with scantily clad bimbos far outnumber images of real women motorcyclists at the controls, attired in riding leathers.

Biker chic, B movies, biker rags—just where *do* real women motorcyclists fit in?

According to Women in the Wind founder Becky Brown, "There's a patch that says, 'Real women ride motorcycles.' The real woman who rides is independent, daring, confident, nontraditional. She's a tomboy, yet she can also be feminine. We're like women who ride horses. We can't do it in a dress."

CHAPTER FIVE

The mere act of riding a motorcycle isn't enough for some women. They like to do it faster than most humans and on a very grand scale. The place they go to indulge themselves is that great American proving ground, the drag strip.

Zoom and the Art of Motorcycle Madness: Women Who Drag-Race Harleys

Women who love Harleys compete in the "all-Harley drags." Their bikes are highly modified for the sole purpose of straight-line, gut-wrenching acceleration. Women who earn professional and semipro licenses can eat up a quarter-mile in half the time it takes to read this sentence, at speeds ranging from 125 to 180 miles per hour.

The all-Harley drags are motorcycling's hot-rod subculture—a world where rubber is burned, fuel is consumed, and engines are strained to their limits for the sake of an adrenaline rush that lasts six to twelve seconds.

The earth rumbles with vibrations that would easily tickle a Richter scale. The ears are assaulted by a deafening roar when carbureted V-twin engines are jolted with electrical charges and flooded with fuel and air, triggering a cycle that has barely changed in a hundred years: Suck in oxygen, dump in fuel, compress the mixture, explode it with sparks, and shoot the waste out the exhaust. And with the crankshaft spinning and pistons stroking, repeat the

OPPOSITE: **A spectacular burnout. Lori Volmert Francis shows the boys how it's done.**

cycle many thousands of times per minute. Nostrils sting, eyeballs burn. Rippling waves of heat rise from the asphalt.

This colorful world is nothing short of a spectacle. Back in the paddock, or "pits," scores of long, low, modified Harleys (FL Big Twins and XL Sportsters) sit under canopies. All the mechanisms of this world are BIG— BIG cylinders, BIG pistons, BIG, fat tires. High hopes ride on high dollars invested in the professional and semipro machines. They are custom-built, often by backyard mechanics, the collective products of thousands of hours of labor and love.

The women who advance to the semipro and professional ranks are Nervy with a capital N, Audacious with a capital A, Competitive

Linda Jackson of Columbia, Missouri

with a capital C. They gotta be. These women wrap their torsos around giant Roman candles, hang on for dear life as they bullet into the void, and push-push-push in pursuit of the win. There's nothing subtle about what they do. In drag-racing jargon, they drop it or dump it (the clutch, that is), then gas it, slam it, hammer it, or gun it. It's WFO—wide friggin' open—on that throttle.

To do this, they gotta have a "dead man's switch"—a breakable tether connecting one wrist to the engine's kill switch. If they fall off and go flyin' and the bike goes flyin', they want that high-revving motor to shut off FAST. They gotta have a wheelie bar—metal rods attached to the chassis that extend five or six feet behind the bike. Wheelie bars keep these rockets earthbound upon their violent launch.

There are different competitive levels or classes. To go really fast—above 150 miles per hour—they gotta have a professional fuel bike, a motorcycle with an engine that drinks nitromethane cut with methyl alcohol. If this sounds like scarey stuff, it is; methane is a type of rocket fuel used by NASA. To go really, *really* fast—above 170 miles per hour, maybe close to 200—they gotta have a fuel bike with a motor that is injected with the stuff; the age-old sucking and mixing of carburetion is too *sloooow*. The 120- to 140-octane gasoline that feeds bikes in the pro and semipro gas classes is for fillies content to trot down the strip at 125 to 155 miles per hour. Amateurs peaking at 100 to 115 in the sportsman or bracket divisions might as well walk.

But everybody's gotta start somewhere, and years ago it was in the sportsman classes that four women—Doris Wiggins, Pam

Cathy "Cat-Lou" West was the first woman to compete in the AMRA in the mid-1980s and has been a fixture at the Harley drags ever since. With a chain from her nose to her ear, West has as much of a "custom" look as her Top Gas machine.

Cummings, Lori Volmert Francis, and Linda Jackson—cut their teeth before climbing the ranks. In this world of overkill, each woman had one of three things: a nickname, a name for her bike, or a name for her race team.

Baby Doris was forty-two-year-old Doris Wiggins, a hairstylist from Clayton, North Carolina. Wiggins became the fastest woman on a Harley when, in August 1992, she soared down the strip on a nitro-injected Super Pro Fueler. Hellraiser was the name of Pam Cummings's race team. Cummings, thirty-seven, a police records supervisor from Waukeegan, Illinois, raised hell a few months earlier among the "good ol' boys" when she became the first woman to race a carbureted nitro bike. Lady Thunder was what *Harley Women* magazine dubbed Lori Volmert Francis, a thirty-five-year-old homemaker and mother from St. Louis, Missouri. Beginning in the late 1980s, Francis became one of the sport's most formidable, repeat national champions in the Pro Stock class, astride a simple, gasoline-fed Sportster. Quarter Queen was the gas-fed Sportster that helped make Linda Jackson a queen of the quarter-mile in the Modified semipro ranks. Jackson, forty-nine, a graphic arts supervisor from Columbia, Missouri, was a rookie at the start of the 1991 season and a national champ by its end.

What kept these women coming back was the euphoric but visceral thrill of acceleration and the idea that they, mere humans, could harness this power and seemingly defy the laws of physics. The faster they went, the stronger those feelings.

Said Doris Wiggins, "The nitro bike is such an awesome piece of machinery, I get such a rush to think I'm gonna ride it."

"I get butterflies in my stomach before every race," said Pam Cummings. "When you're in a jet plane speeding on a runway and the ground becomes a blur, that's what it feels like on a nitro bike. You're going so fast, just a little more and you'd be flying."

With all its noise and huffing, puffing machinery, drag racing may seem full of

Pam Cummings

machismo, but the motorcycle is truly an equalizer. For all the sport's swagger, you don't have to be a Schwarzenegger to ride a rocket.

**Cummings on the starting line atop her carbureted V-twin rocket;
photos of dragster cars inspired the bodywork.**

Even the mildest Lois Lane can transform herself into Superwoman, and Pam Cummings was living proof. "I used to be so meek," she said. "I was fat from age five until I was twenty-one. Other kids, including my four brothers, made fun of me. In school, no one wanted me on their team."

In her late twenties, Cummings was introduced to drag racing by her (now ex) husband, a motorcycle mechanic. She said, "At first, I asked myself, 'Are you just seeing how far you can go, or are you trying to prove something?' It felt good to push myself to my limits, beat other people at a sport, and do something better and faster than my brothers."

Sometimes, being better and faster had a price. In a decade of drag racing, Cummings sustained her share of broken bike parts and fractured bones. "Not only was I the first female to get on a nitro bike, I was the first one to explode a nitro motor, in May 1993," she said.

With such tremendous forces placed upon the engines, various mishaps—due to mechanical failure or, occasionally, pilot error—can explode a motor or destroy other vital systems. Metal parts may shoot right through the engine cases like shrapnel.

Cummings explained, "My stock [original factory] engine cases couldn't withstand the pressure. I was about a hundred feet into my run when the cylinders blew and ripped the fuel line off the tank. Nitro sprayed out and a piston shot sixty-five feet in the air. What a mess! I was covered with nitro and oil—good thing there was nothing around to ignite me." Unlike race car drivers, motorcycle racers do not wear fireproof suits because they are not

Linda Jackson with John, her husband and crew chief, and the Quarter Queen, their Sportster propelled by a 74-cubic-inch powerplant. They later upgraded the engine.

Jackson on the line

enclosed. Cummings escaped injury that time because the bike simply glided to a halt.

The gentle Linda Jackson had thrown herself into the sport as a means of coping with a devastating loss, the death of her only child. Jackson's daughter had multiple birth defects, including blindness and cerebral palsy. A former Special Olympics wheelchair racer, the girl died in 1991 at the age of nineteen.

Jackson used to exude an aura of melancholy. She recalled, "For nineteen years, I devoted my life and all of my energy to my daughter. When she was taken from me, I felt very alone. I asked myself, How do I socialize with people when all I've known is my relationship with my child and my husband? Drag racing was healthy because I could absorb myself in it. The tension of the competition, the attention paid to me, the curiosity of people in the pits—all of it was new. The sport got me in front of people and turned a lot of things around."

But Jackson, too, paid a price, in the form of a freak accident in 1992. While she was going 115 miles per hour, a bolt on her bike's swingarm (the arm attaching the rear wheel to the chassis) broke. The bike slid on its side. Jackson hung on for a second—long enough for the clutch lever to gouge a couple of fingers before she let go and tumbled for 240 feet. Yet she was back on the track in eight weeks to defend her number-one plate.

The women insisted their sport was safe compared to other forms of motorcycle competition—they were in their own lane, going straight, and done in seconds. They shrugged off the risks, saying they "come with the territory."

Much has been documented on the physiological effects of speed on the human mind and body. Extreme acceleration produces an intense state of arousal, which some people experience as terror, a throwback, perhaps, to a primordial "fight or flight" response. But others get a pleasurable thrill. Either way, the crux is adrenaline.

Richard Wegner, president of the American Motorcycle Racing Association (AMRA), a ten-year-old organization that sanctions all-Harley drags in the central United States, has seen thousands of people in the grips of the fever. He put it this way: "The feeling produced by acceleration gets into your blood. The pursuit of it causes people to give up their jobs, mates, social lives, and anything else that stands in the way of feeling it again."

Fortunately for our intrepid women, the all-Harley drags *were* their social life, sponging up all of their vacation time and most of their disposable income. But they hadn't forsaken their mates. Having a husband (in some cases, a father) for a crew chief was almost *required* in order to advance in this fraternity.

Many women in the professional and semipro ranks grew up in families where the smells of gasoline and motor oil were as common at the supper table as Ma's home cookin'. Many were their "father's daughters." Doris Wiggins's dad pumped gas. Pam Cummings's father owned a gas station/repair shop where she and her brothers worked. Lori Volmert Francis grew up racing dirt bikes on a flat track with her father, brother, and cousins. Linda Jackson's dad, who raced stock cars, "had a little bit of gas in his blood."

The women tended to marry motorheads. These men loved building bikes and experimenting with their creations while their wives served as test pilots. The husbands were usually dyed-in-the-wool Harley men—members of what was perhaps the most "macho" subculture in motorcycling. And yet, like any male racer and his (sometimes female) crew chief, these couples were symbiotic.

Said Doris Wiggins, "When I fly down the strip on that bike that Johnny's worked so hard to perfect, it's his shining glory moment."

"If Ken makes a tuning error, we lose," said Lori Francis. "If he tunes it right, we win when I do my part right. We are a team."

The reactions of less enlightened men were of little consequence to Wiggins and Francis. These women were there to compete, in the dictionary definition of the word: "to seek or strive for something in opposition to others."

Doris and Johnny Wiggins with their Super Pro Fueler, a nitro-injected Big Twin with 300 horsepower.

**Lori Volmert Francis (foreground)
and Cathy West.**

In opposition, certainly, to anyone who dared to ask, "What's a nice girl like you doing on a drag bike instead of doing the dishes?" Both worked at "female" occupations—hairdresser and homemaker—but after that, they parted with tradition.

With her genuine Southern twang, Wiggins declared: "I'm not a woman who likes to shop at malls. It tortures me to go to a grocery store. Motorcycles are my life." Wiggins's clients knew it—she wore Harley T-shirts to the beauty shop, kept a picture of her drag bike on the counter, and readily proclaimed to anyone who'd listen, "I'm the fastest woman on a Harley. When people pick

at me for getting on a nitro bike, I just tell 'em I'm a go-for-the-gusto girl." One of seven children, she grew up competing for attention from the minute she opened her eyes each morning until she closed them at night.

At the drag strip, Wiggins quickly learned to ignore naysayers. "In the beginning, the boys in the gas classes had all kinds of attitudes toward me and my husband. No matter what they said, we weren't leaving. The fuel pilots respect me because they know what it takes to ride a nitro bike."

Lori Francis started drag racing twelve years ago on a dare from a girlfriend and won her first event. Her name has repeatedly cropped up on annual lists of national champions—as often as any of the top men.

"When I started, some guys got their feelings hurt," she said. "It wasn't a female/male thing. I'm a good pilot. I tried to make them feel better by congratulating them on positive things they did, even if I'd done it better. It's not like that anymore. Most of them look at me as a competitor, not as a woman."

Not just *anyone* is invited to run with the big boys. Established pilots and track officials observe an up-and-comer, then endorse her professional license. Drag racing may look easy—just gun the throttle and go hell-bent-for-leather, right? It ain't so simple. If it wasn't a constant challenge, the pros wouldn't keep coming back in search of the perfect pass.

Drag racers compete head-to-head in pairs on an eighth-mile or quarter-mile strip. They start with qualifying rounds or passes. Then, in elimination rounds, slower riders are weeded out until the top guns are left to shoot it out in the finals. Performance is measured by speed (MPH) and elapsed time (ET).

At the starting line is a "Christmas tree," colored bulbs that flash for ready, set, go. The racer has to watch the bulbs in her peripheral vision and "cut a light"—that is, drop the clutch and launch on the yellow, four-tenths of a second *before* the green. If she snoozes, she loses. She must ignore a rival who delays staging (getting ready). This ploy forces her to keep her brain and engine revved in anticipation of the go. Tension runs high at the starting line.

On a gas bike, she must shift at the right

Alabama's Sharon Garrison set eight national records on a Sportster.

RPM or kiss the transmission good-bye. Nitro bikes zoom instantly from idle to top gear. The launch is so violent, they may fly down the track solely on the rear wheel. The pilot, atop a 180-MPH unicycle, has a choice: Keep it straight or crash into a guardrail.

Lori Francis has never tired of the chase: "It's not the speed that gets my stomach twisted, it's the competition. If the other guy's ahead of me, I want more. *'C'mon, c'mon, gimme more, gimme more,'* I say to myself. And when it's over, I'm out of breath. Everybody's huffing and puffing like they ran all the way down the strip. There's no other feeling like it, whether you win or lose."

Florida's Jan Downing. Her drag bike was custom-built at Tampa V-Twin, her shop.

More Power! A Brief History of Drag Racing

Kristine Becker, the first woman to win a nitro class event in the AHDRA.

The concept of drag racing is as American as apple pie. The sport reflects our national obsession with size, power, competition, and the internal combustion engine. Mine's bigger, mine's faster, mine's better than yours. It's loud, boisterous, and crude. It's American.

While humans have probably gone head-to-head in straight-line competition ever since the wheel was invented, more formalized drag racing got popular at least as far back as the 1940s, when World War II veterans took their hot rods to the dry lake beds of California. Bikers who *really* had something to prove went to the Bonneville Salt Flats near Wendover, Utah. There, they lay down in the cramped cockpits of two-wheeled, cigar-shaped vehicles called streamliners. In 1978, stuntwoman Marcia Holly became the first woman to break into Bonneville's 200 MPH Club. Piloting a Kawasaki-based streamliner, Holly set a land-speed record of 229.361 MPH. (In 1985, she set a record in a car of 272.014 MPH.)

Today, motorcycle drag racing takes place at facilities built specifically for that purpose. The American Motorcycle Racing Association sanctions all-Harley drags in the country's midsection. There are about fifteen hundred licensed AMRA pilots. Of these, about two dozen are women, most in the amateur classes. Roughly the same numbers apply to the All-Harley Drag Racing Association (AHDRA), which holds races on both coasts. The East Coast Racing Association (ECRA) is an all-Harley venue in the Northeast.

Harley lovers like to be amongst their own, partially because Harley "lifestyle" bikers share a unique camaraderie. But it's also so that the push-rod V-twins don't have to be measured against other engines.

If you don't ride a Harley, there are drags for all brands of bikes, such as those held under the banner of AMA ProStar. The National Hot Rod Association (NHRA) also has a motorcycle division. At all-brand events, some of the nitro-injected beasts, running on Japanese-based motors, take about six seconds to rocket through the quarter-mile at well over 200 MPH.

In 1995, at age 16, Kersten Hopkins became the youngest female nitro pilot ever.

If you're interested in getting your feet wet, consider ET handicap or bracket racing. Basically, you tell the starter how many seconds you'll need to reach the timing lights, then try to match that time. See the appendix for addresses of drag race organizations.

ROCKET WOMEN: SHOOTING STARS OF THE ALL-HARLEY DRAGS

Saturday, June 12, 1993, was the day that Doris Wiggins—fastest woman on a Harley—set her personal best. She did it at a drag strip in Union Grove, Wisconsin, at an AMRA meet in front of thousands of spectators. It was much more than a typical drag-racing weekend. Just twenty miles north, roughly a hundred thousand motorcyclists had converged in Milwaukee to celebrate the ninetieth anniversary of the Harley-Davidson Motor Company. To race Milwaukee Iron that weekend was to be a part of history. The all-Harley drags had a gritty, down-home feeling. The bleachers were filled with Harley "lifestyle bikers"—lots of bearded men in black T-shirts and leather vests, some with club colors (insignias).

About 250 drag racers—whom AMRA head Rich Wegner dubbed "the most awesome Harley racers on the planet Earth"—had come to test their mettle. Of these, at least eight professional and semipro pilots were women. The list read like a Who's Who of the best in the sport. Besides Wiggins, there were Pam Cummings, Linda Jackson, and Lori Francis. Top contenders Sharon Garrison of Alabama, Jan Downing of Florida, and Vicki Johnston of Tennessee had made the trip. So had Indiana's Cathy "Cat-Lou" West, the first woman to compete in the AMRA. And there were several amateurs in the "run whatcha brung" classes.

On Saturday, when the call sounded for the injected fuelers' qualifying rounds, Wiggins pulled on her leathers, tucked her red hair inside her helmet, and climbed aboard her King Kong of a motorcycle. She joined the line of pounding hearts awaiting their turn to fly down the quarter-mile strip. Her Super Pro Fueler looked like a giant praying mantis sculpted from purple metal. The chassis was made of chrome moly, an alloy lighter but stronger than steel. It was eighty-four inches long from axle to axle, and with a six-foot wheelie bar extending from the rear, the whole contraption was almost as long as a dragster car. On the frame above the engine, her nickname, "Baby Doris," was delicately scripted.

But there was nothing delicate about this thirty-thousand-dollar machine, built by her husband and their friend, legendary pilot Bill "Godfather of Fuel" Furr. The bike was an ultimate power tool: 113 cubic inches of Harley's Evolution motor, doctored to churn out more than 300 horsepower. (In its original factory state, it had 60 hp.) A nine-inch-wide rear tire, treadless or "slick" for maximum grip, would carry this rocket down the dragstrip.

But not before the burnout, a critical step that the racers took to get that tire hot and sticky. The burnout doubled as a ritual display of power that transfixed the crowd perhaps more than the racing. And nobody enjoyed it more than Doris Wiggins, the queen of overkill, the self-proclaimed "go-for-the-gusto girl." At the signal from a track official, Wiggins told herself, *"It's showtime!"*

She straddle-walked the bike in front of the burnout trough, a wet depression in the ground where she would spin the rear tire to generate friction. But first, Johnny connected an off-board starter mechanism to the bike's crankshaft. Doris flipped the ignition and the motor

Doris Wiggins on her revamped nitro bike: same engine but shorter chassis.

kicked over with such fury that the torque (rotational force) flung the connector out.

Johnny pushed the bike back so the rear wheel was in the water. Doris grabbed the front brake and opened the throttle. The engine bellowed, and as it reached an ear-splitting crescendo, the back tire spun, melted, and blew up a cloud of black smoke. It appeared that Doris Wiggins was astride a mythical, fire-breathing dragon. The smoke, the noise, and the stinging smell of nitro and burnt rubber formed a booming cascade, like the aftermath of fireworks.

Wiggins eased off the front brake and let the beast lunge forward about ten feet for a "short hop." Satisfied that her tire had a good bite, she straddle-walked the monster to the starting line, where Johnny helped her line up straight.

Wiggins was lying down on the frame above the bike's twin combustion chambers. Her short arms were barely able to reach the hand-grips. With her eyes dead-set over the handle-

bars, she concentrated fiercely while her rival delayed staging, hoping she'd lose her edge.

Fat chance. At the yellow light—four-tenths of a second before the green—Wiggins dropped the clutch, opened the throttle, and launched in spectacular fashion. With her front tire airborne a few inches, she roared down the strip on the rear wheel. In 7.9 seconds, she flew past the traps (timing lights) at 172 miles per hour. Through the adrenaline rush, she sensed what Johnny saw on the boards: She had made it into the "sevens." It was her personal best and she qualified number one for the next day's elimination rounds. Back in the pits, Wiggins chuckled, "It's a good thing I have a lot of hair 'cause my head does get big."

On the following day, Sunday, June 13, Pam Cummings strutted her stuff. This formerly overweight girl was now a platinum-blond woman with a spikey punk haircut, tall and svelte in a white leather suit. Astride a white, arrow-shaped drag bike with a carbureted, 99-cubic-inch nitro motor, she ran nose-to-nose with a rival, zooming past the traps at 154 miles per hour in 8.8 seconds. Cummings lost by one-*hundredth* of a second, but she'd made a perfect pass. It was nirvana, her fastest run ever. An awestruck woman came up to her and blurted, "Gosh, girl—when I watch you, it makes me proud to be a woman!"

Linda Jackson didn't fare as well in her Modified gas class. She experimented with new engine heads, which caused her motor to bog. Pro Stock champ Lori Francis moved up (temporarily) to Top Gas. Problems with her chassis and rear tire almost veered her into a guardrail, but she refused to pack it in. It took Bob Taft, peaking at 157 MPH on the world's fastest Top Gas Harley, to eliminate Francis. And then there was nothing left to do but see if Doris Wiggins would top her own personal best.

Wiggins did outgun herself. She soared through the traps at *175* miles per hour in 7.9 seconds, traveling more than eighty-five yards per second. Upon deceleration, her front wheel touched down and then—suddenly—her front tire skidded. Wiggins lost control. She flew up and over the handlebars, landed on the ground, and was knocked unconscious. The motorcycle was wrecked. Later she said, "Another pilot had raced in that lane just before me. His motor exploded and dumped oil at the finish line. My front wheel hit it."[1]

Wiggins sustained a serious concussion, lost her memory for five days, and couldn't get back on the bike for two months. She wasn't fazed: "I just love racing this bike. It's like rid-ing a horse. Ya gotta get back on if you fall off."

Pam Cummings fell off her horse two weeks later. While cranked up to 125 miles per hour at the end of an eighth-mile strip, Cummings was blown off course by a 40-MPH crosswind. Hitting a rut, she and the bike were flung up in the air. The wheelie bar struck her leg and broke it. The following year, Cummings divorced her crew chief and had to sell the bike. She pit-crewed for a funny-car racing team while dreaming of piloting another nitro bike.

In the months to come, Doris Wiggins hit the pavement again, less harshly, but never quit. "I've done my body-slamming bit," she insisted. "I'm determined I'm gonna get the best of these motorcycles and not vice versa." In 1995, she had a shorter chassis built, one more within her reach and in a color more suited to a "gusto girl"—hot pink.

Meanwhile, the other women were still pushing the envelope in the AMRA. In a single season, Sharon Garrison set eight—count 'em, eight—national speed and ET records, and captured the Number One plate in Super Modified XL. Linda Jackson swept both national and regional championships in her class of '95. That same year, Lori Francis set a Pro Stock record of 158.4 MPH and placed second in the nation.

Like surfers waiting for the perfect wave, these denizens of the drag strip were forever searching for the perfect pass, that zone where concentration was so intense, where human reaction synergized with motion and the innards of the machine. The perfect pass. These women had found the thing that made them feel most alive, and they just did it.

CHAPTER SIX

A select group of women partake in the ultimate challenge: road-racing motorcycles on asphalt circuits, competing amongst men at breathtaking speeds.

Europeans began road racing after World War I, when motorcycles were slow enough to steer on public courses that webbed through countrysides and villages. But as machines became faster and faster, zooming through populated areas was too dangerous.

The sport then moved to closed outdoor circuits that mimicked the winding roads, and thus kept the name "road racing." In America, today's asphalt courses are designed for the brave, with banked corners, switchbacks, hills, and dips. In between, there are straightaways where

Road Warriors: Women Who Race Superbikes

the most high-tech machines can rocket from 150 to nearly 200 miles per hour. One lap is akin to a two- or three-mile roller-coaster ride. A sprint race may last a few laps, with a pack of jockeys vying to the finish. Endurance contests last from two to twenty-four hours; the longer races are relays, in which team members take turns on one bike.

Some racers describe the sport's feeling in the jargon of addicts.

"What a high!"

"It's such a rush!"

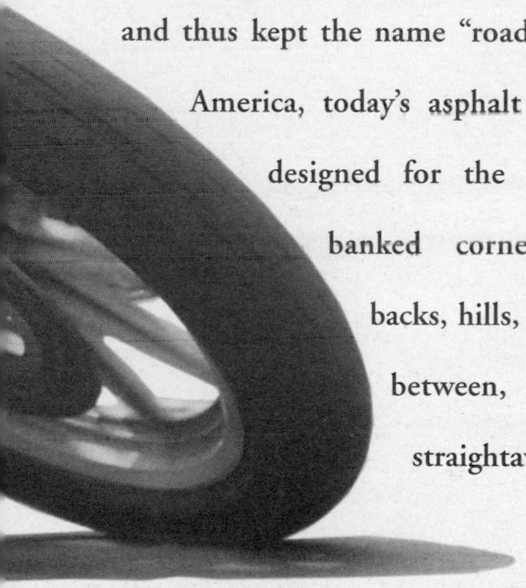

OPPOSITE: **Nancy Delgado on a Harley Sportster, hailed as a prototypical superbike.** (Brian J. Nelson/Euro Tech)

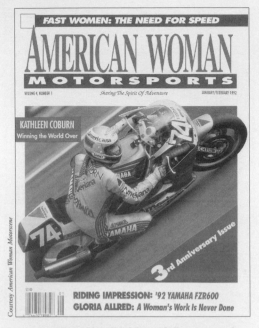

FAST WOMEN: THE NEED FOR SPEED

AMERICAN WOMAN
MOTORSPORTS

VOLUME 4, NUMBER 1   Sharing The Spirit Of Adventure   JANUARY/FEBRUARY 1992

KATHLEEN COBURN
Winning the World Over

3rd Anniversary Issue

RIDING IMPRESSION: '92 YAMAHA FZR600
GLORIA ALLRED: A Woman's Work Is Never Done

Courtesy American Woman Motorscene

ABOVE: Canadian Kathleen Coburn raced internationally in the late 1980s. "I was different from other women," she said. "I didn't want to be a girl doing well for a girl. I wanted to win." She had major factory sponsorship until childbirth put her on the sidelines.
BELOW: Delgado spent her first two years as a pro (1991–92) aboard Sportsters.

Like a hang glider, sky diver, or any other athlete who partakes in an "edge" sport, a road racer in the height of her passion is close to death yet most vibrantly alive. With pilots zooming toward hairpin curves at such high speeds, some argue that road racing is the riskiest motorcycle sport. Perhaps not coincidentally, women who advance to the pros tend to be single and childless.[1] But they aren't crazies with a death wish.

"They have a life wish, a desire to live life to its fullest." So says psychologist Frank Farley, a Ph.D. from the University of Wisconsin who has studied risk-taking behavior in a variety of people, from parachutists to entrepreneurs. He calls risk takers "Type Ts," for "thrill seekers."

Says Farley: "Type Ts feel their destiny is in their own hands, so they like to be in situations where they can act. They are usually self-confident, independent thinkers motivated by risk, intensity, and the unknown. The motorcycle offers a lot to this person."

A woman who road-races a motorcycle is a

Brian J. Nelson/Euro Tech

technician with a specialty in speed. On a superbike, she straddles a primeval fault line: her need to survive versus her need to take risks. With such a whirlwind pace—at 120 miles per hour she covers 176 feet per *second*—there is no room for error. But if she hesitates and brakes a half-second too early in a curve, she's lost her edge and, perhaps, the race. In endurance contests, there's some leeway, since there's time to catch up.

Women who dare to enter this sport do so as underdogs. They are usually too old (in their twenties) by the time they qualify for a spot on the grid among men who have greater strength to muscle the machine, not to mention the advantage of social conditioning and phys-ed curricula that instill aggression and dominance into boys, but not girls. Further, very few parents will let girls compete on the rough-and-tumble dirt track, where most road-racing champions get their start. As adults, women may race with no family encouragement; some nail-biting parents can't bear to watch.

On the track, minor to moderate fractures, sprains, and contusions are common. The occasional high-speed crash into a barrier can be crippling, or fatal, despite the best helmet and padded leather suit. Tragedy does *not* strike often, but to brush it off as "rare" would be a lie. Every road racer knows of someone who's paid a price.

In the United States, most asphalt tracks are modern and well maintained, but in the early nineties, this wasn't exactly true of Ohio's Nelson Ledges Race Course, home of the grueling 24 Hours of Nelson Ledges, a quarter-of-a-century-old event. By Inde-

pendence Day Weekend 1993, endurance racers who braved the deteriorated circuit wore the experience like a badge. This was the story of a rare, all-woman team of privateers who competed in the 24 Hours that weekend. The women worked with a shoestring budget in the middleweight superbike class, where almost any performance modification to a factory bike was allowed.

TWENTY-FOUR HOURS OF GRIT

In the midst of the rural blackness near Garrettsville, Ohio, there was a primitive racetrack with no overhead lighting. The hot July night was pierced by the sound of thirty-four engines screaming at redline. Over and over the motors cranked up to 11, 12, 13,000 RPM, wound down a few grand, and shot back up to their limits. It was near midnight and the riders had been doing this—blasting away on the straights and braking hard into the corners—since three o'clock in the afternoon.

ABOVE: **Racers on the starting grid at Nelson Ledges Race Course in Ohio.** BELOW: **Endurance team members,** FROM LEFT, **Letha Jeffers, Nancy Delgado, and Cathy Creighton.**

The scene on Nelson Ledges Race Course was almost surreal. Thirty-four halogen headlights flew around the course like bodiless spirits, because behind the lights you could barely see the bikes. The riders crouched behind their windscreens could barely see the track: Mist, dense fog, and smoke from spectators' campfires obscured their vision, making every lap a leap of faith.

The two-mile track was so badly broken up that the 24 Hours of Nelson Ledges was Darwinian—it was not so much a race that year as survival of the fittest. It was a test of which riders could keep the rubber down through incredible fatigue, which pit crew could keep the bike assembled through a day and night of bolt-rattling, tire-splitting ripples, bumps, and potholes.

Circling the course in the midst of this madness was a headlight attached to a black Yamaha FZR600 superbike. The pilot was

The race is suspended while workers clear the track of debris, one of many times that accidents or bike failures among the thirty-four teams stopped the action. As Cathy Creighton pulls into pit lane, crew chief Teri Sabin is ready to service the bike.

Letha Jeffers is about to race for another hour.

Letha Jeffers, captain of the nation's only all-woman endurance team. Jeffers was an ex–rugby player turned gardener and mechanic. A lanky six feet one, she had a weathered face, tired eyes, and a deep Virginia drawl. At thirty-eight, she was the oldest rider on the six-woman team. She was a motorhead who lived and breathed bikes.

Jeffers had barely slept since before the previous day's long drive to the track. While speeding, she scanned the course for oil and errant toads and critters from the surrounding swamp. Toad-kill, not to mention larger roadkill, could be awfully slippery stuff to a tire. The poor visibility forced her to concentrate so fiercely that she blew past riders who usually passed her in the daylight. Nothing existed beyond the bike and the next curve ahead. This was what she lived for, this

state of speeding, altered consciousness.

Jeffers thundered toward a corner at about 120 miles per hour. She clicked down a gear or two and hit the brakes firmly, slowing to perhaps 70 or 80. Centrifugal force and inertia tried to fling the bike straight off the track, but Jeffers fought the laws of physics by shifting her weight to the inside of the turn. Hanging off the speeding bike, she stuck out a padded knee and dragged it on the ground with a *chrrrrrrrrrrrr!* as the bike swooped into the corner.

She was leaned way over—her head was only a couple of feet from the ground—and in a flash she was at the apex of the curve. With eyes focused at the exit of the turn, she shifted her weight up, pivoted the bike, upshifted, and drove hard onto the straight. In the pitch-black night with the engine howling, she felt that *rush* as the speedo hit 130 miles per hour and then—*phffftuh!*—the sudden splat of a flying insect on her helmet visor, right at eyeball level, tweaked her consciousness.

Back in the pits, Cathy Creighton, Jeffers's friend and cofounder of the women's team, was so wired she couldn't sit still. The top half of her one-piece leather racing suit was pulled down to reveal a tank top. Creighton strolled pit row with the arms of the suit dangling at her back. The humid air smelt of fuel, oil, solvents, sweaty leathers, and mud from the previous night's rain. People milled about beneath the line of colorful canopies. Some sat on lawn chairs or coolers filled with Gatorade and beer. Tools and spare parts

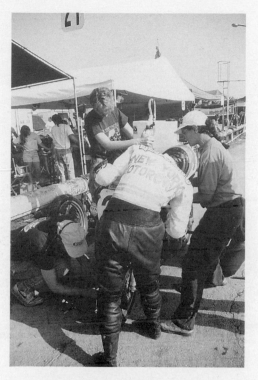

The crew descends upon the bike in a typical pit stop.

A rival team's booster message.

were everywhere. At least one crashed motorcycle was being pieced back together.

Creighton was itching for another hour on the FZR. At thirty-two, she was an admitted "adrenaline junkie" who cross-trained by running, lifting weights, swimming, and occasionally riding motocross bikes with her enduro champion boyfriend. Creighton was five feet eight, as wholesome looking as an Ivory girl, and made her living as a sous-chef. She learned to race a decade ago while studying culinary arts in England. She checked her watch as the clock ticked into July Fourth. Jeffers was scheduled to come in soon, so Creighton headed back to her team's pit and zipped up her racing suit.

Having slept for about an hour, Delgado cools off while awaiting her turn to race.

Jeffers rolled in and was barely out of the saddle when the crew descended upon the bike. In about forty seconds, two men and two women dumped in four gallons of gas, topped off the motor oil, adjusted and lubed the chain, and scanned the bike for loose nuts and bolts. Then Creighton, wearing amber glasses behind her helmet visor, rode out into the blackness.

Past the front straight, she glided out from under the pedestrian bridge and was blinded by a billowing cloud of black smoke from the track's diesel generator. At about 110 miles per hour, Creighton couldn't see a thing, but she was prepared. The night before, she had walked the track and planted reflective tape on key braking and turning points. "There's my dot!" she exclaimed with relief as she steered through the bog.

In a few seconds, she entered a tight, 180-degree horseshoe with ripples in the pavement. Creighton muscled the bike to hold her line as the FZR pogoed through the corner. Twelve hours around this obstacle course had squished the bike's shocks, but it had not put a dent in the team's determination.

They'd started with six riders. Newcomer Danielle Saxman, stricken with a stomach virus, withdrew early. Just before dawn, an eager Alanna Davis sped into a corner too hot, crashed, and went home with minor injuries. By sunrise, the team was left with four riders, two of whom had been up all night. The amateur pit crew spent well over an hour patching up the crashed bike.

In the morning, Nancy Delgado was the first to go out on the rolling wreck. At twenty-eight, the sloe-eyed Delgado looked more like a waif than the most tenacious woman ever to storm road-racing tracks in this country. She was small boned yet flicked the four-hundred-pound bike with fluid, almost balletic maneuvers as she weaved past slower competitors.

Delgado had raced many bikes since a boyfriend introduced her to the sport in 1987, but she learned to muscle a big machine in 1991. That year, she turned pro aboard a five-hundred-pound Harley Sportster 883 and was the only woman in the AMA Twin Sports Series. To qualify, Delgado lifted weights and built herself up from ninety-eight pounds to one hundred ten. To master the art of sliding, she cross-trained in winter by ice-racing a dirt bike with metal-studded tires.

Early on, she learned that competition would be fierce against a few men who resented her presence. "There were guys who said they wouldn't go home if they didn't beat me," she recalled. "Another guy introduced me to his sister as the token female. I said, 'Hi, I'm the token female who always beats your brother.'"

In one rookie race, Delgado taped a bikini-clad calendar pinup to the back of her bike. The guys ogled the photo and she crossed the finish line first. From then on, her in-your-face attitude enabled her to survive in the sport but made some rivals bristle. Delgado used her gender to get noticed by the press. Though her track record was respectable compared to most male privateers, at times even better, it wasn't always the stuff of champions. Some guys whined, "Why should *she* get the ink? If she was a man, they'd ignore her."

Delgado's response: "I benefited from my own PR efforts, got exposure for the sport, and opened doors for other women." In-your-face.

Her first year on the Harley ended when another rider crashed into her, hurling her against a concrete wall. Delgado sustained a fractured skull yet got back in the saddle the next season. When she wasn't networking for sponsorship, she cleaned houses to support her passion and relax her high-strung nerves.

On this day at Nelson Ledges Race Course, as Delgado circled the bumpy course in the seventeenth hour of the race, she held steady at one-minute, sixteen-second lap times. That was four seconds off the lead pace, but by then it didn't matter—her goal was to keep the sagging machine in one piece to the end. So she stayed out of trouble, finessing and forcing the FZR to do her bid-

The FZR has been leaking oil; Delgado, still wearing her back protector, inspects the bike with Creighton.

Euro Tech

ABOVE: Delgado on the FZR.
BELOW: Candace Gregoire.

ding in this choreographed production that was part ballet, part bullfight.

The next rider up was Candace Gregoire, a New Hampshire novice who mustered 1:25s in her first endurance race. The FZR had been leaking oil since Alanna Davis's predawn crash and the fluid was dripping down Gregoire's leg. The rookie didn't know the source and hoped—no, prayed—that the slick stuff would stay off her tires.

At eleven A.M., the bike in the neighboring pit came back charred from a blowup. The crash left the rider with minor injuries and the race was suspended while cornerworkers cleared debris from the track. Jeffers and her pit crew changed the last of three sets of tires on the FZR.

Creighton rode out the twenty-fourth hour. The field had slowed down to a leisurely cruise—thirty-four riders dearly wished to see

The wearisome task of counting laps and recording lap times. Teri Sabin does it all.

twelfth in the middleweight superbike class and twenty-eighth in the whole field.

In privateer road racing—where the phrase "labor of love" was often stretched to dogged lengths—these women on their shoestring budget and ragtag schedule had just broken through an awesome gender barrier. They proved to the guys they were typical.

A track official strolled by and said, "Good job, ladies!"

"We suck and you know it," replied Creighton.

"We're not this bad," Delgado chimed in. "You should have seen us last year. Fourth place."

IN THE YEARS TO COME . . .

Each woman remained active in the sport as a racer or instructor. In 1995, Nancy Delgado became the first woman to win a championship in the new National American Superbike (NASB) series, aboard a 125cc grand prix bike. (She also posed for *Playboy*.) Candace Gregoire advanced to the expert ranks on a 125 at her home track in Louden, New Hampshire. Letha Jeffers opened her own repair shop. Cathy Creighton studied radiology and retired from competition, exclaiming, "I dedicated my last race to my mother, my boyfriend, and everyone who ever wanted to see me quit!"

the checkered flag from an upright position. Finally, at three P.M., they did.

A pasty-faced Creighton rolled into pit lane and dismounted. Quietly, her brother David handed her a beer. While some back-slapping and whoops could be heard down pit row, Delgado and Gregoire were expression-less. Andrea Brady, Jeffers's roommate, was shooting the scene on video. Jeffers mounted the bike, raised her arms in a V, and cried, "Thank you for not blowin' up!"

After a race that had seen countless bikes scraping, bouncing, and careening across the rough pavement, the women had completed 848 laps, or 1,696 miles. This put them

If rodeo cowgirls had wheels instead of horses, they'd race motocross. Because it takes one hell of a rider to wield a dirt bike weighing 150 to 230 pounds as it bucks and bounces through ruts, bumps, and dips. It takes a hell of a racer to slide the bike deep into a hairpin turn, whip the back

Cowgirls on Wheels: Women Who Race Motocross

end around while using one leg as an outrigger, power up a fifteen-foot hill . . . then launch the bike off the peak and land, as one coach has said, "as if you're jumping from a

two-story window." And it takes a fierce competitor to do this as fast as she can in a pack of like-minded loonies, most of whom are men.

Motocross is a wild, physically demanding sport. It is a mix of rodeo and steeplechase—except that the "jockeys" ride dirt bikes with springy suspensions and tall, knobby tires. Women and girls who race in the high-flying mud are fresh-faced jocks—the most athletic women you'll find astride motorcycles. For much of the race, they stand on the footpegs, leaning forward. With elbows up and out, they balance and vault their bikes over obstacles. They use muscles many of us don't know we have.

The word *motocross* (MX) combines "moto," short for motorcycle, and "cross," for cross-country. The sport originated in post–World War II Europe, where open country served as the track. It came to America in the 1960s and was popularized

OPPOSITE: **Women motocrossers let loose from the starting gate.**

by Steve McQueen's 1971 documentary, *On Any Sunday*. The American Motorcyclist Association, the sport's premiere sanctioning organization, says motocross has been the fastest-growing form of motorcycle competition in two decades.

Today's outdoor motocross courses are closed circuits carved into natural terrain. They are generally a half-mile to a mile and a half in length. One race is comprised of two or three heats called motos. One moto can last anywhere from four to twelve laps and take ten to twenty minutes. Whoever finishes the best of two or three motos is the overall winner.

If the landscape is too tame, sadistic designers create obstacles for your riding terror. The wooliest sections have nicknames like Ten Commandments, Gravity Cavity, Animal Leap, King Kong, and Twin Peaks.

Respectively, these names denote a washboard section of whoops (large bumps), a crater-sized dip, two tabletop hills or launchpads, and a double jump. There are potholes, rocks, hairpin turns, wide sweepers, and berms (banked shoulders). Mercifully, there are also straightaways. On a long enough straight, a pro rider on a 250cc bike may top out in sixth gear at about 60 to 70 MPH, which is very fast in the dirt.

But in this sport, it's not how fast you can go, it's how far you can fly. The main attractions of motocross, and its indoor cousins, arenacross and supercross, are the spectacular double and triple jumps. Like acrobatic daredevils, the best riders fly their bikes over two or three hills. On average, the hills are ten to fifteen feet high; the total length of a double or triple jump can reach anywhere from

twenty to sixty feet or more. Riders say jumping a bike is a "rush" or "natural high."

Retired national champion Mercedes Gonzalez of California, the dominant female motocrosser of the late 1980s and early '90s, excelled at indoor supercross. As an amateur in the United States, she was a consistent top-three to top-five finisher; internationally among pros, she placed top five to ten. Teenager Kristy Shealy of Houston, Texas, aspires to do even better.

Motocrossers and supercrossers fall down a lot, sometimes on top of one another in a pile-up of spokes and limbs. Even the AMA once quipped: "Motocross is the black-and-blue division of motorcycle racing." Although jockeys wear plastic armor, minor to moderate injuries are common. But they get so hooked, some still race with fractured fingers or broken ribs.

Motocross has drawn the widest age range of any motorcycle sport. Strikingly, children old enough to ride a bicycle without training wheels can start in the "peewee" classes on mild little tracks. The kids ride 50cc mini-bikes with automatic transmissions; without modifications, they can go up to about 25 miles per hour. Skilled adolescents graduate to 80cc machines, which are occasionally allowed in the same rugged field as larger bikes. There are veteran classes for riders over thirty, forty, and fifty, and events for owners of vintage bikes.

As in other types of motorcycle racing, women are a minority, yet there are probably more of them racing amateur motocross on a regular basis than any other type of motorcycle competition. Since the sport often runs in families, this is one likely reason.

Many women and teenage girls ride 125cc bikes, which are light enough to throw around yet powerful enough for hard competition. A handful of the most aggressive women also race heavier 250cc machines. There are no dilettantes in this class. These femme fatales have honed their skills by hammering with the men and boys every weekend. When these women vie against one another, their contests are as fierce as any men's race.

But as in other sports, venues for women are few and cash rewards are almost nil. This is controversial. A fledgling movement of female promoters want the industry to sanction separate women's classes. Some men are receptive, but most believe that there aren't enough "fast" women—or women, period—to make it cost-effective. Novices intimidated by the idea of racing with men may never enter the sport, so there will never be more than a few women—"fast" or otherwise.

The big question is: Who sets the standards for "fast"?

Every year in August, the lines are redrawn at Loretta Lynn's Dude Ranch in Hurricane Mills, Tennessee. This is the site of the prestigious, AMA-sanctioned Amateur and Youth National Motocross Championships. Out of twenty-eight classes, there is only one that pits women against women. The AMA has considered dividing the field, but for now, all are lumped in the same field. Novice girls, intermediates, and over-thirty veterans are at the gate with young pros. The pros lap the field; that is, they complete a lap so fast, they pass the stragglers. At other venues, the serious women go out against the men and admit it

At age eleven in 1993, Heather Matthews was the youngest rider to win a women's national event, on a Kawasaki KX60.

forces them to go faster. It's "kill or get killed." But, as in asphalt road racing, men—with greater strength, aggressive social conditioning, a serious phys-ed curricula, and generally an earlier start in the sport—have an edge. In a mixed field, the odds against women are great.

A recent article in *American Motorcyclist* magazine declared: "It's not written anywhere, but there is a pyramid to climb at the Amateur Nationals. . . . Why do these riders and their families devote so much time and money to racing? One powerful motivation is the invisible pyramid, the promise of a factory ride."[1]

It's not visible to the naked eye, but at the top of the pyramid is a sign that says, GIRLS NEED NOT APPLY. Beyond her pride and love for the sport, there is little motivation for a girl or her family to strive toward the male standard of "fast." The factory scouts are watching the boys.

Kristy Shealy, who may grow into the fastest woman motocrosser of all time, said, "It's unfair that there's only one women's class, but we can't say anything 'cause they'll get mad at us and not have a women's class at all."

Tami Rice, a longtime California motocrosser in her mid-thirties, never cared who got mad. While racing, she spent years banging at the dirt ceiling, insisting, "Women of all skill levels have the right to compete and be rated against their peers. Why should motocross be any different from tennis, golf, or the Olympics?"

In 1988, Rice formed a league, later called the Women's International Motorsport Association (WIMSA). With local promoters, she hosted several championship meets that drew forty to one hundred riders. But with tepid

Tami Rice, daughter of motocross pioneeer John Rice, started riding dirt bikes at age five.

industry support and some feathers ruffled by her outspokenness, WIMSA stood on shaky ground.

I n *The Stronger Women Get, the More Men Love Football*, author Mariah Burton Nelson wrote:

We can read, on a daily basis, stories told by men about men: male strength, male bonding, male power and struggle and sweat. Imagine if we could also read stories told by women about

Racers Shirlyn Smith (foreground) and Brenda Yancey of California

women: female strength, female bonding,

female power and struggle and

sweat. What if, in the sports pages, we

could read how a friendship is chal-

lenged and strengthened when two

women compete for one position? . . .

What if we saw, on a daily basis, female

athletes in action, muscles taut, faces

intent on victory? [2]

This was the story of one woman's campaign to get the industry to recognize the
heights that women in motor sports could
reach, rather than to minimize their abilities
by stacking them against the opposite sex. It
was a day in the life of female strength, bonding, power and struggle and sweat—in a different venue: the hills, dips, bumps, and ruts
of the motocross track.

A LEAGUE OF THEIR OWN

In the wee hours of the morning of May 29,
1994, the sky above Oklahoma City was
astreak with lightning. Thunder shook Tami
Rice awake from an overwound sleep. Then
came the rain in torrents. Flash floods washed
out roads and the red clay track of Motorcycle
Raceway turned into a a quagmire of earth-
sucking mud.

The first World Cup championship races
of the Women's International Motorsport
Association were to take place on this day. As
wind gusts rattled the bedroom window,
Rice—promoter, motocrosser, and president
of WIMSA—had a tough time fighting back
tears. This stormy Sunday was the culmina-
tion of Rice's seven-year struggle to wrest one
day a year of track time from the men, so that
women could go head-to-head in a series of
heats separating novices from pros.

While working as a lab technician in the
late 1980s, Rice had formed WIMSA. She
had a meager budget, no business savvy, little
industry backing, and, three years later, a
newborn son. A single mother with boundless
nervous energy, Rice tried to carve a niche in
the old-boy motocross network while child
rearing and commuting to work.

"I'm very competitive," said Rice. "Motorcycles are a power thing. All these years, I've
heard women aren't supposed to do this, but
I've proven they can."

Her WIMSA World Cup in Oklahoma
was one of only two such events on American
soil in 1994. Kat Spann, publisher of the
monthly *Tex-MX News,* hosted the other one
two weeks later in Texas. That was *it* for the

whole year. Eight female racers—women *and* girls—from Russia, the Ukraine, France, Australia, and New Zealand journeyed with their trainers and families to compete against the Americans.

Rice hosted the foreigners at the track owner's Oklahoma City home. Starting at four A.M., as the rain kept pelting and the thunder kept booming, one by one the bedroom lights came on.

"This is good weather for my girls," said Leonid Majorov, the brawny coach of the Moscow team. The Aussies quipped, "This rain is nothing."

And so, by seven A.M., an international caravan of windshield-wiping, dirt bike–laden vans inched its way across flooded highways toward the track. And then, almost eerily, the rain stopped. The course at Motorcycle Raceway looked like a construction site after a landslide. Axle-deep in mud, a tractor heaved the earth until it loosely resembled a motocross course.

Meanwhile, Rice set up a registration booth for the racers who braved the squall. She hung banners and lined up the victory plaques to await the winners. Then it hit her: She had staged a field of dreams for women who love motocross and forty of them had come, despite the hazardous storm. They had come for love of the sport—certainly, not for the purse. A thousand dollars was all she could muster, to be divided among winners in several classes.

As the skies gradually cleared, pit row began to look like a cross between a vast aerobics studio and a parts swap meet for Japanese dirt bikes. Pitwear for these

motocrossers was closer to jockwear: Besides T-shirts, the younger women sauntered around in gym tights and stretch halter tops that doubled as sports bras. There were lots of mud-caked sneakers.

These were the same women who, on the starting line, covered in protective gear, kickstarted their engines and thrashed at this gritty sport. These women were literally tough as nails—some had surgically implanted metal splints on various bones, the results of hard crashes. These motocrossers had pushed the envelope of athleticism, proven their ability in a "guy's sport," mastered—gasp!—*machines,* and gotten dirty doing it.

At noon, after a three-hour delay, the course was opened for practice in the mud. The women donned their armor, looking genderless beneath the padded plastic. Their helmets, jerseys, pants, and bikes were painted in startling fluorescent colors—the stuff was bright enough to land an airplane by.

After a brief practice, the races began. The woman to watch was the defending champion, twenty-five-year-old Dee Ann Wood of Dallas, Texas, who raced in the 125cc and 250cc pro classes. At five feet nine and 130 pounds, Wood was one of the fastest women motocrossers ever. Disarmingly, she was also one of the shyest. Mighty Mouse—the cartoon character on her helmet—summed up the contradiction that was Dee Ann Wood. A green-eyed brunette with long, wavy hair, she once prompted a male racer to shout, "That girl's faster 'n shit! She's faster 'n *me!*"

Wood had been raised on frequent doses of encouragement from her Harley-riding mother, who said, "Never be afraid to try anything. Who says girls aren't supposed to ride?" And so, at three, Wood got on a pint-sized Indian painted with stars and stripes like Evil Kneivel's stunt bike. At nine, she raced cross-country, then switched to motocross at fifteen.

At the time, Mercedes Gonzalez was the dominant female motocrosser. Wood couldn't catch her before quitting to shoot hoops on a

basketball scholarship at Midwestern State University in Texas, where she earned a B.A. in business administration. "Basketball gave me the chance to be a leader," she said. "The game was intense and my teammates became like sisters. The bonding helped me cope with my greatest loss." Wood's mother died from breast cancer in 1990.

After college, Wood managed her father's Harley franchise near Dallas. "When basketball ended," she said, "I had to have something competitive and physical to focus my energy on, or I would've gone crazy." She returned to motocross and "got my chance at beating Mercedes." Gonzalez retired in 1991

at the age of twenty-eight, losing her last moto to Wood at Loretta Lynn's.

Wood's success was all the more phenomenal given her limited practice time. She rode dirt bikes mainly at night and cross-trained by weight lifting, mountain biking, and running. She earned a truckload of trophies and sustained numerous injuries. Her talent and perseverance earned her modest support from Kawasaki and some local business owners.

The deciding race in Oklahoma, and the one most telling of Wood's mettle, was the second moto of the 125 pro class, a come-from-behind affair at the end of the day. Her chief

Dee Wood of Dallas, Texas. Her plate number says it all.

Gale Webb: "Just Say MX!"

"Motocross is better than drugs" is the message purveyed by veteran racer and sports evangelist Gale Webb. Her jersey is emblazoned with the words MX MOM. With her bleached, cropped hair and ruddy complexion, Webb is over fifty but going on fifteen.

Gale Webb

She is also the survivor of a near-fatal skydiving accident. At the age of twenty, when her main chute failed to open, Webb sustained massive head injuries, a broken neck and back, partial paralysis, memory loss, and learning disorders. She spent the next two years in a hospital but her rehabilitation has been a lifelong process.

She used sports—motocross, snowboarding, skiing, and mountain biking—as physical and emotional therapy. She fought doctors and inner demons who told her she'd never lead a normal life. "I was always wild," said Webb. "When they told me 'you can't,' I did."

Corina Chinen

"America's Sports Mom" is a role she invented for herself in the late 1970s. After her best friend died from a drug overdose, Webb became an antidrug crusader. With help from her husband and grown son, she stages sports shows at fairs, parks, and malls. Her troupe of young bicyclists, in-line skaters, and skateboardists roll, flip, and leap to music while Webb cries, "Kids! You don't need drugs to have fun! Get high on sports!"

Corina Chinen, twenty-five, who began riding dirt bikes with her father in the pineapple fields of their native Hawaii, agrees with Webb. Said Chinen, "The sensation of flying a bike in the air is a natural high. Motocross keeps you focused. You have to stay healthy or you're going to get hurt." While working as a production assistant in her father's construction firm, Chinen saved money so she could come to the mainland and train for the pros.

Dee Wood soars off a tabletop jump.

opponent was Michaela Gonzalez, a thirty-three-year-old software engineer from Colorado Springs, who'd been racing since childhood.

Fourteen riders were called to the gate. By then, the rain-soaked ground had semi-coagulated but was slick as ice in spots. Speed alone couldn't win on this track. It would take skill, nerve, and endurance.

Wood's green eyes were piercing as she put on her steely "race face." The riders pulled on the last bit of protective gear, the bulbous goggles. Then they looked like superhero characters. At the first signal from the gatemaster, the women kickstarted their engines and the air reverberated with a loud, raucous sound. Were these motorcycles or kazoo-powered lawn mowers?

At the next signal, they shifted into gear and revved those little motors until they screamed. There wasn't a gut not aflutter, a vein not nearly bursting with adrenaline. These pumped-up jockeys on their neighing metal ponies were ready for the chase.

It was the holeshot they were after, these jockeys. The holeshot—the lead into the first turn—can make or break a race. Be first around that hallowed corner or close behind the leader, and you're in it to possibly win it. Get caught in the midst of the pack, and you may never break out. Except if you're Dee "Mighty Mouse" Wood.

The gate dropped and the jockeys blasted off in a cloud of red dust. Wood got caught in the middle. Michaela Gonzalez got the holeshot and hung on to the lead. "Mighty Mouse" turned into a lioness in pursuit.

Wood weaved through the pack, commanding the inside line through turn after turn. Like a boxer, she watched for weakness in her opponents, then darted through. She charged until she was at Gonzalez's tail, pushing her front wheel into the leader's peripheral vision. Wood's technique was visceral. She launched hard off the hills, landed hard on the flats, charged hard into the corners, and skimmed the ground with her pivoting leg as she whipped the back end of the bike around. It was a beautiful sight.

But Gonzalez was stubborn. For six rowdy laps, she blocked Wood and held her to the outside of the corners, then dusted her on the straights. The women battled until they came to a 180-degree turn. Gonzalez left an eyelet for Wood to bullet through. The two bikes shrieked as they raced down a straight and bucked over the whoops. Wood lunged her bike forward and then, in a sudden lash of momentum, she roosted Gonzalez. The checkered flag flew for Wood.

Tami Rice, watching from the observation tower, had goosebumps. "The level of competition was amazing," she said. "It was also a personal victory to realize how far WIMSA had come. But then I remembered the brick walls. Why hasn't the industry accepted that women can do this?"

By the end of the WIMSA World Cup in Oklahoma City, Dee Wood had swept both the 250cc and 125cc pro classes, defending her title as world champion.

The storm before dawn, the quagmire at the track, the ploughing through, the gradual clearing, and, finally, the success of the event, were a miniseries of Tami Rice's struggle to put women's motocross on the map. By the end of the year, flailing under a pile of debts, Rice was forced to fold WIMSA. Afterward, she taught women to race and helped promote local meets.

Yet on this day in Oklahoma City, as the legendary Mercedes Gonzalez handed out plaques to winners in eleven competitive classes, there was an unspoken sense that the World Cup had been a milestone.

Return of the Racers

In the 1970s, motocross was even more popular among young women than it is now. A California group called PURR (Powder Puffs Unlimited Riders and Racers) sanctioned its first "Powder Puff Nationals" in 1974. According to a newspaper account, there were more than 150 entrants and "the intensive training programs of the experts, including jogging and weights, produced top-notched athletes." But not for long—most women sat out the eighties. Male resistance, marriage, pregnancy, and the skyrocketing cost of bikes kept many on the sidelines.

Today, women are back on the motocross track and they've brought their daughters with them. Debbie Matthews, thirty-eight, from Mission Viejo, California, competed in the Powder Puff Nationals. Now she races in the over-thirty veteran class and is working to continue what Tami Rice started.

With Elaine Ruff of Acerbis, USA (a motocross equipment maker), and two other colleagues, Matthews manages the U.S. Women's Motocross League, a descendent of WIMSA formed in 1995. Ruff's industry experience and connections have helped her and Matthews make inroads where Rice had faced road-blocks. "Tami helped pave the way for what we are able to do," Matthews said. "She had the heart but not the tools. We saw the obstacles she faced and developed strategies to get around them."

Besides the new league, Matthews and Ruff manage the U.S. Women's Motocross Team, comprised of the top four racers, who may change every year. Team members receive corporate sponsorship and represent the United States in international competition.

The league may herald a boom in women's motocross. "We already have eight hundred members," said Matthews. "At our championships, we've had to turn girls away at the gate." In 1996, the league received an AMA charter and thus a guarantee of AMA sanctioning for league events. This victory is a first step toward gaining wider industry support for women's motocross.

It comes not a moment too soon for girls like Matthews's fourteen-year-old daughter, Heather, who began 50cc "peewee" racing when she was seven. Heather got knocked down five times in her first moto; undaunted, she finished the race. While growing up, Heather was easy to spot on the track. The antenna sticking up from her helmet was a giveaway. Using an intercom and hand signals, Debbie Matthews coached the child from the sidelines. Raising her fists, Matthews cheered, "C'mon, Heather, you can do it!" On a typical day, a boy rival's father would yell, "Johnny, don't let that girl beat you!" His wife might counter with, "Go, Heather!"

At age twelve, the resilient child began racing an 80cc bike, sometimes in the same field as her mother. Debbie Matthews said, "The sport gives the kids goals. It keeps 'em off the street and out of trouble."

Veteran racer Debbie Matthews (center) shows her trophies with daughter Heather (foreground) and peewee racer Jillian Bennett. When other mothers asked Matthews how she could let her daughter compete in such a rough sport, Matthews said, "I don't think she should be held back just because she's a girl."

CHAPTER EIGHT

"*My worst nightmare came true! I was in a construction zone, and as far as the eye could see, it was ankle-deep in gooey mud. Well, 'Mush, baby, mush!' I got through the first eight hundred feet. Then my arms got tired of fighting the handlebars and my legs gave out from dragging the mud and trying to keep the Harley up. I didn't really drop her—I buried her! I had mud up to my knees with splatters all over me and a gob on my face. What a bath! I loved every minute of it.*"

—**Amy Mullins, sixty-two, recalling her solo ride through the Canadian Yukon**

"*I was riding through sand trails in Costa Rica and came upon a river. I couldn't tell how deep it was and there was no other way to pass. I was nervous. I thought, I can't get the bike through, I'll have to turn back, which is against my religion. Then a local man came by and waded through. The water was knee-deep, so I plunged the bike in and made it across. I felt like that song, 'I am woman, hear me roar!' I can do anything! I can have grandchildren! I can cook! And I can ford rivers! It was a hoot!*"

—**Catharine Rambeau, sixty-one, recalling her solo ride through Central Amerioa**

Flying Solo: Adventurers and Explorers

Some women use their motorcycles to go beyond the controlled environment of the racetrack ... beyond the local roads of a Sunday jaunt with friends ... away from the hangouts where bikers meet to kick tires.

These women want none of that. When they go out on their motorcycles, they go

OPPOSITE: Amy Mullins geared up for a rough ride on the Alcan Highway (Amy Mullins Collection)

Amy Mullins Collection

For Mullins, riding north on the Alcan from Haines Junction, Yukon, toward Alaska was like taking a giant mud bath.

into themselves. They ride alone and very far. As much as racers live on the edge, these women push their personal envelopes by embarking on long, solo flights to unknown places. Going in, they know that hardship and danger are likely to rear up as often as exhilaration and freedom. They get off on the mixture.

Amy Mullins, a retired power plant technician from St. Clair, Michigan, and Catharine Rambeau, a magazine editor and former film critic from Lantana, Florida, were two such women. Both divorced many years, both grandmothers, both stubborn. Far from retiring into the empty nest, Rambeau and Mullins were propelled by a relentless energy.

In the late 1980s, both women set aside the time and some modest resources to fulfill their dreams of adventure. They were never tourists. They were *travelers,* drinking in the highs and lows in a manner true to the original meaning of the word: *travail.*

NORTHERN EXPOSURE

What brought Amy Mullins to leave home in July 1988 and, for the duration of the month, to slosh and bounce her 650-pound Harley Low Rider up the infamous roads of the Canadian Yukon and the Alcan Highway to Fairbanks, Alaska? What goaded this five-foot-one, 110-pound woman to tackle what many

Amy Mullins Collection

She made it!

bikers say is one of the two last, great overland adventures on the continent? (Inuvik in the Arctic Circle, the northernmost point on the continent accessible by land, is the other.)

"I did it for the same reasons people climb mountains—for the sense of accomplishment," said Mullins. "I'd already ridden all over the country, so going to California on a motorcycle was no big deal anymore.

"I didn't just want to see Alaska," she continued. "I wanted to *ride* it. The north country is not like civilization as we know it. Up there, you are a real adventurer. The country reaches out and grabs you, especially on a bike."

Mullins was in her early fifties at the time

of the trek. She was (and still is) a walking powerhouse who lifts weights in competition and rock-climbs with her grown son. Mullins's inner and outer strength stood her well up north. Much of her journal read like this:

The rocks thrown up by passing trucks could rearrange your front teeth.

The last stretch of road before the Alaskan border was a terror. The frost heaves (buckled road) were so bad, I hit

Amy Mullins Collection

A peaceful moment at Kluane Lake, Yukon

the frame of the bike a couple of times. I

really white-knuckled it through there.

She concluded: "It was *all* positive because I glory in that kind of challenge. It was worth it to see the crystal glaciers, the wildlife and landscapes so vivid, it looked like God had taken a paintbrush and dipped the land in color."

Years of self-sufficiency and resourcefulness had prepared Mullins for the rigors of the road. "I used to have a house where the toilet got clogged. A plumber wanted fifty bucks to clear it. I said, 'Forget it.' I took the toilet out of the floor and got the obstruction out. From

Readin', Ridin', and Rallyin'

At the end of every May for the past several years, Cindy Earle dismissed her fifth-grade students for summer recess, while Dan, her college professor husband, wrapped up his semester. Cindy packed her BMW K75S with camping gear while Dan loaded his van with canoe and kayak. They kissed good-bye and locked their house in Baton Rouge, Louisiana. Except for brief sojourns when their paths crossed, they didn't see each other for two months. She rode America's roads; he navigated its rivers.

Earle, in her fifties and the mother of a grown daughter, made a loop of the continent that typically traversed more than twenty-five states and a Canadian province or two. She saw old friends at a dozen BMW rallies and the Women on Wheels Ride-In. She won several long-distance mileage awards.

Her ongoing travels have been a study in extremes: The loneliness and monotony of the interstates have been relieved by the camaraderie of the rallygoers and explorations of scenic back roads. And yet, one of Earle's favorite encounters occurred in the midst of monotony.

"My itinerary forced me to ride I-70 through Kansas four times," she recalled. "I thought, Surely, there must be something that changes in Kansas. I needed to have a memorable encounter with someone other than having a meal and buying gas."

Cindy Earle

Nature provided the answer: an impending tornado. "I figured *now* would be the time to get my bike serviced." Earle pulled into a repair shop, where she exchanged laughter and road stories with another stranded rider. "It was a three-hour encounter while the storm passed. Now I love Kansas."

Many of her interstate miles have been meditative. She explained, "It's a good time to look at yourself and learn from your actions. Riding helps me keep my head on straight and it puts the stresses of school on hold. [She teaches underprivileged and some troubled youngsters.] The road shows me how to live *each day* and to view every moment as a gift. June and July on the road alone are my summer celebration."

Catharine S. Rambeau Collection

Catharine Rambeau rode "Mojo," her Honda XL250S, from the United States to the southernmost village in Latin America.

there, I started working on houses." Mullins designed her own home, did most of the plumbing and all of the wiring.

"The older I get, the more independent I get," she said. "I always travel alone because it's my time to do what I want. All your life you're confined; people set rules you have to obey. On my vacation, I want total freedom. Then I'm not gonna come home and cook dinner for any man."

Her next goal is Inuvik or bust. A true Harley lover, she may do it on a Sportster because "it's only five hundred pounds. If I drop it, it's light enough to lift by myself."

SOUTHERN ODYSSEY

Catharine Rambeau was fifty-three and the mother of a grown son when she embarked upon her South American odyssey in 1988. But she learned the most important thing she needed to know for that trip when she was twelve.

"One day my mother drove me and my brothers to the dentist," Rambeau said. "The roads were slick from a frozen rain. Suddenly, the car went out of control and spun around three times. My mother simply turned off the ignition and waited till the car calmed down. Then she smiled and asked, 'Is everybody all right?' She switched the car on, turned it the right way, and continued to drive. She never made a scene, never cried. Just took care of business. Thirty-five years later, I realized that what I'd seen had changed my life."

Like her mother, Rambeau became a woman who always took care of business. Whatever came up, she *dealt* with it. When faced with the choice of losing weight or

spending the rest of her life as a diabetic, she shed eighty-six pounds. In the summer of 1988, the magazine she worked for closed its doors. "I was out of work for the first time in decades. I'd saved some money and decided that now was the time to pursue a serious adventure, my reward for thirty years of hard work."

Rambeau combined her interest in Latin culture with her love of riding. She obtained her mother's blessing, drew up a will, and rented her house. That December, she left Florida on a used, 250cc Honda dual-sport (on/off road) bike with a kickstarter.

For Rambeau, there was no other choice but to go on a motorcycle. "In a car, you're a self-contained unit. You can even eat in a car. The bike meant I had to reach out to people. I had to ask how far to the next gas station? Where could I sleep? Is this road dangerous?"

She continued, "When you travel long distances on a motorcycle, it's you and the road, you and the machine, you and the weather. It's your decisions and your mistakes. When something unexpected happens, you make an adventure of it. A nut that's not properly tightened on the bike can be an introduction to a whole village. If you take that attitude home to family and work, everyone is enriched."

Rambeau's crash into a boulder in Ecuador and her failed attempts to ride the bike over the crest of a steep, sandy hill (with help, she pushed it over) were among her unplanned "adventures." She navigated roads that were thrilling and terrifying, like that mountain pass in Colombia—altitude: eleven thousand feet. "I was so high up, I was in the clouds,

Catharine S. Rambeau Collection

In 1916, pioneer rider Adeline Van Buren said, "On a motorcycle, all roads lead to the end of the world if one has but the courage to follow them." On her 250cc Honda, Catharine Rambeau followed this road, literally, to the end of the world. This desolate portion of the Pan-American Highway is so high in the Colombian mountains, it is shrouded in clouds.

In 1993, FROM LEFT, Leenie Bachman, Doris Buksa, Gin Shear, and Sue Slate rode from the Atlantic coast to Inuvik in the Arctic Circle. Gravel, steep grades, and washouts caused a flat tire and "moving dismounts." Here, they relax at the Chuk campground, Northwest Territory, Yukon. Although they rode eighteen hours that day, Slate said, "When it's light at two in the morning, the child in you comes out."

Women's Motorcyclist Foundation

surrounded by their wetness," she recalled. Mist obscured her vision of the narrow road while cloud matter swirled through the spokes of her wheels. "It was a stiff haul and there were no guardrails, no margin for error. I was so scared, I sang "Amazing Grace" to myself because I thought I was going to die." But she *dealt* with it.

The Latin newspapers were intrigued by her moxie and a string of stories preceded her arrival in many villages. "I hated being defined as a motorcycling grandmother," Rambeau said, adding that her happiest times were the forty-four days she spent riding the high, cool Sechura and Atacama deserts, of Peru and Chile. "In the desert, there were no definitions. Everything was so stripped down, so lacking in falsity. There was a moment when I was able to disappear into the road. When I 'came to,' as it were, I'd forgotten the day, the month, even where I was. I'd forgotten my age, my sex, my color. I was just this creature.

It was a wonderful, freeing experience. The only expectations were mine."

A year after leaving home, when she'd ridden to the far, far underside of the globe, Rambeau fulfilled those expectations. She sat by herself, sipping wine and watching a late sunset over the Beagle Channel, where Charles Darwin had once sailed. Quietly, she celebrated the end of an arduous journey that had taken her through South American war zones, rain forests, and cobblestoned streets to where she was then: Argentina's most southern outpost—Ushuaia, a village on the island of Tierra del Fuego known as the end of the world. Local officials verified that Rambeau was the first woman to make the trek from the United States alone on a motorcycle.

Naturally, the first person she called was her mother.

Through tears of pride Rambeau exclaimed, "Hey, Ma! I made it! I bleeping made it!"

A Woman and Three Wheels

"People with disabilities can do an awful lot," said forty-six-year-old Marsha Wacker. Indeed, she should know.

Due to a birth defect, Wacker had both legs amputated above the knee when she was only one year old. With a wise mother who "never told me I wasn't supposed to do things," Wacker embarked on a life of exploring the possibilities. Today, this Cleveland, Ohio, resident is a vocational counselor to teenagers with disabilities—and a motorcycle sidecarist, downhill skier, and kayaker. She walks with artificial limbs and travels in a modified, 1000cc Moto Guzzi California II with a sidecar. Beaumont, her begoggled standard poodle, is her frequent passenger.

Marsha Wacker and Beaumont

Wacker has driven the sidecar rig on roads that would challenge sport riders even on nimble two-wheelers—from the Rocky Mountains and the Oregon coastline to remote trails in Nova Scotia. She has never let her disability limit her horizons. "I'm adventurous," she said. "I really want to live life, and the motorcycle has given me a life I wouldn't have otherwise. I can't run or ride bicycles. But with the motorcycle, I'm on the same plane as a person who is able-bodied. I can enjoy the wind in my face."

She has come a long way from the nineteen-year-old girl who—against great odds—learned to ride a two-wheeled, 90cc Honda. "I have free-swinging knees, so when I stopped the bike, I lost my balance. I fell over so many times that my key was bent in the ignition. But I allowed myself to fall and then figured out another way."

That way was to add a third wheel. She is a certified sidecar safety instructor who says, "It's exhilarating to handle the sidecar rig in the twisties at speed." Deal's Gap at the Tennessee/North Carolina border—three hundred and eleven curves in eleven miles—"was just incredible. I know I'm good and I push the edge of what the bike can handle."

Echoing common sentiments among women who ride, Wacker added, "I've had so many great moments on the motorcycle. Plus I enjoy the independence."

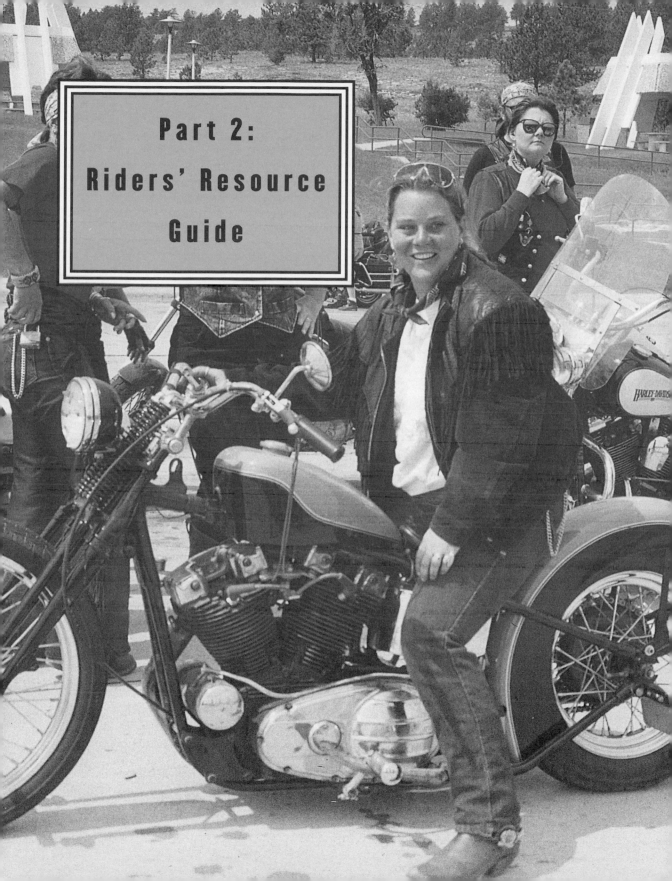

Part 2:
Riders' Resource
Guide

Motorcycle rallies are places where the sport's subcultures mingle. They are ad hoc cities—gatherings of tribes where motorcyclists from all rides of life are brought together by their passion for two-wheeled travel. The larger rallies are fun, fascinating panoramas of

A Biker's Social Calendar: Rallies, Runs, and Watering Holes

all the strata within the motorcycle community. They are places for tire kicking, camaraderie, and, of course, riding.

Sometimes, members of different motorcycle camps coexist but do not exactly mingle. In extreme cases, brand loyalty is so strong that some groups are snobbish toward outsiders. There are exceptions to every rule, but rallies are also laden with stereotypes, and it can be astounding to observe the lengths to which adults go to label one another.

Rallies range from fewer than five hundred people at a local one-day meet to two hundred thousand or more at a long-established national event spread over a week or so. The largest rallies offer amateur competitive riding events, parties, custom bike shows, scenic tours, informational seminars, shopping, demo rides of new bikes, professional races, and more. Smaller affairs have less of everything—including fewer hassles and fewer crowds.

Basically, the calendar consists of rallies geared to various groups: Harley riders, owners

OPPOSITE: **Main Street in Sturgis, South Dakota, during the Black Hills Motor Classic**

Vera Griffin Collection

Vera Griffin Collection

This motordrome or "Wall of Death" near Daytona dates back to the 1930s. Women have always been motordrome stunt riders. Here, Nita Nielsen rides the wall and Betty Fritz practices standing in the saddle, both circa late 1930s or '40s.

of other specific brands, owners of luxury touring bikes, women riders. There are events for other groups and lots of overlap. Rally addresses are in the Directory.

HARLEY-ORIENTED RALLIES

The Season Opener: Daytona Bike Week

The social and racing calendars begin in late February in Daytona Beach, Florida, with Bike Week, considered a rite of spring. Bike

Week has grown to about eleven days of festive and competitive events held within a twenty-five-mile radius of the town's Main Street. Although much of Bike Week is geared to Harley lovers, increasingly, riders of all brands have been coming to Daytona. They trek from all across the continent, even if it means trailer-towing their bikes through winter's chill. Typically, an estimated two hundred thousand people attend.

Main Street is a bikers' Mardi Gras, *the* place to see and be seen. The Harley-Davidson lifestyle is on parade. All day and into the wee hours, Harley riders cruise the crowded street. Many bikes are artwork-in-motion, with their gleaming chrome and custom paint jobs. During the evening party hours, the rumble and roar of thousands of Harleys, many with straight (unmuffled) pipes, can be deafening and so intense that the ground vibrates. Interspersed among the "hogs" are a few riders on plastic-covered Japanese and Italian sport bikes, BMWs, British bikes, and huge touring rigs.

While recovering from the blinding glare of all the chrome, occasionally the eye rests upon an archaeological dig-on-wheels. These are the beat-up rat bikes, dinosaurs that lumber along in proud defiance of Harley's Evolution motor, not to mention upscale Evolution bikers. A true rat bike is akin to a homeless person's shopping cart, replete with the trappings of a nomadic life. Cooking and camping utensils, arcane spare parts, and anything else from deer antlers to vintage memorabilia may adorn a rat bike.

The sidewalks and shops of Main Street are packed with bikers in denim jeans and leather vests. Most of the men appear to be auditioning for the same part in *Masters of Menace*, with their requisite beards, black T-shirts, potbellies, and tattoos. The majority of women in jeans and tank tops do not get photographed; the few in bikinis always do. There are also "profilers" and "rubbies" (rich urban bikers) in designer leathers. Depending on your point of view, the scene is awesome or a parody.

Away from Main Street, there are dozens of activities. At the Volusia County Fairgrounds, you can wander among the rust of an old-fashioned parts swap meet. At the Ocean Convention Center, you can sample the latest Harley-Davidson accessories and Motor-Clothes. You can wade through crowds at the Rat's Hole Custom Motorcycle Show. Here, practically every other machine is a radically chopped-out Harley with a skull or death gas tank mural. Voluptuous women, flames, demons, and Native American themes are also de rigueur. And if female coleslaw wrestling is your thing, Daytona has it.

The circus that has become today's Bike Week is a far cry from its humble beginnings, which lie in racing. In 1937, the original excuse for bikers to come here was the Daytona 200. Jocks raced their machines on the beach. In the early sixties, the race was moved to a closed-circuit asphalt track. Today, only a fraction of Bike Week attendees watch the races at Daytona International Speedway, which culminate with the 200. The attitude of some Harley lifestyle bikers is summed up on a T-shirt that says, "Fuck the races. I came to party."

In the speedway pits, the jocks downing

Bike Week in Florida: Motorcycles take over Daytona Beach.

Gatorade couldn't care less about Main Street. They do not consider themselves "bikers." They are "motorcyclists" who are here to see mostly foreign-made superbikes zoom around the high banks of Daytona. The visceral roar of these rockets blasting on a straightaway at 170 MPH can send chills up the spine.

Twenty miles north of Daytona at the Bulow Campground in Flagler Beach, another subculture of "motorcyclists" gathers. Every year, the local Space Coast BMW Riders Club reserves a chunk of the campground for "Beemer" owners and their guests. For two bucks, any rider (on any brand of bike) is welcome to a homey breakfast of pan-

cakes, coffee, and camaraderie. The camp is disarmingly quiet because BMWs don't roar.

It is often said that Daytona represents a clashing of cultures, but perhaps it is not so much a clashing as a juncture. Hoping to build on the popularity of Bike Week and create "a more family-oriented rally," a few years ago, organizers started Biketoberfest, a smaller event in the fall.

Sturgis Rally and Races: Thunder in the Hills

Tucked in a valley at the foot of South Dakota's Black Hills, there is a sleepy town called Sturgis, with a population of about

Sturgis draws bikers from all over the continent and a few from abroad. As one person put it, "On a motorcycle, you can go anywhere and find this common ground."

seven thousand. But for one week every August, that number may swell to two hundred thousand as bikers converge for the Black Hills Motor Classic, also known as the Sturgis Rally & Races. Like Daytona, Sturgis draws mostly Harley owners with a smattering of other riders.

Here, too, Main Street is a mecca, but the ambience at Sturgis is different. On the oil-soaked street, the undulating sea of leather, denim, and chrome has a rougher edge. Amongst the friendly lifestyle bikers, 1%er clubs are more visible. They keep mainly to themselves, but most years, a bar brawl or two makes the news.

For the duration of the Classic, local shopkeepers rent their stores to vendors selling leather, bike parts and accessories, silver jewelry, bandannas, greasy food, coonskin hats, and Nazi regalia favored by hardcore types. There are pins and patches that sneer "Die yuppie scum" and "If it has tits or wheels, it will give you trouble." The hardcore element frequents certain campgrounds. In some sections, the atmosphere can be so raunchy that unescorted women are ill-advised to enter. At every turn, drunken men blurt, "Show your tits." Some sit next to signs that say the same.

While these elements can be found in Daytona as well, they are more blatant at

Sturgis. Yet despite the sharp edges, the rally is what you make of it. If you love bikes, especially beautifully customized Harleys, and if you are fascinated by humanity in all its diversity, it's worth braving the gridlock to partake in what the local papers have dubbed "a Woodstock in leathers." Even the late billionaire biker Malcolm Forbes was a Sturgis fan. Several times in the 1980s, Forbes beat the traffic by floating over it—in his seventy-five-foot-high hot-air balloon, shaped like a Harley, of course.

At Sturgis, you'll meet two-wheeling crusaders for Christ and Brothers of the Third Wheel on trikes. For five bucks, you can have your picture taken with a six-foot snake on your shoulders. You can get a tattoo or sit on a curb and hear stories from old, grizzled bikers, nearly all of whom are named Pappy.

In fact, it was a local motorcycle dealer named Pappy Hoel who, with the Jackpine Gypsies Motorcycle Club, started this affair on a small scale in 1938. They held races on a dirt horse track and led bikers on scenic rides. Over the years, the event grew and changed for better and worse. Old-timers say that before the Vietnam era, the crowd was "cleaner cut." Today, only a fraction of rally-goers attend the dirt track races, though the all-Harley drags are quite popular.

Ladies of Harley member Jean Livermore shows her Heritage Softail at a HOG Ride-In Show. Custom touches include gold plating, a solo seat, snakeskin handgrips, and, of course, chrome.

Closeup of some radical paint at Daytona's Rat's Hole Custom Motorcycle Show

Activities around the area range from rock concerts to the *Harley Women* magazine Ladies Day Ride and Party. At bikers' amateur rodeos or field meets, riding skill and sense of humor are equally tested. Serious contenders race their machines around barrels and ride through cone weaves. For laughs, there is the infamous weenie bite for couples riding two-up. A hot dog slathered in mustard is hung from a rope suspended between two posts. As the driver passes beneath the dog, the passenger attempts to bite off a chunk. The biggest bite wins.

Many people come to Sturgis for what lies beyond the town. In the Black Hills, roads wind through spectacular landscapes. You may pass buffalo roaming a prairie. Nearby are Custer State Park, Mount Rushmore, the Crazy Horse Monument, and the Badlands, a geological wonderland of colored canyons and spires.

Laconia, the Granddaddy of Rallies

Every June in the days leading up to Father's Day, New Hampshire is the site of Laconia Rally & Race Week, a smaller version of Sturgis. Estimates on the typical number of attendees varies widely, from twenty thousand to an optimistic one hundred fifty thousand. The scene unfolds along a small boardwalk at

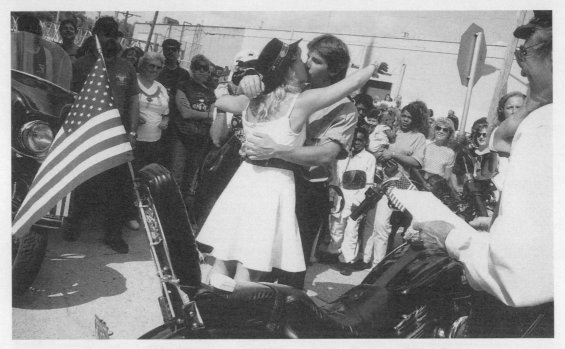

A biker wedding in front of 3700 West Juneau Avenue in Milwaukee. If you don't recognize that address, you wouldn't understand.

Weirs Beach on the shore of Lake Winnipesaukee. Problem is, since only a single, two-lane road leads to the area, it may take two hours of clutch-grinding and straddle-walking to inch your way in. The locals sit on lawn chairs to gawk at the stalled parade of bikes.

The Laconia rally originated in the 1920s, making it the oldest event of its kind. But Laconia, too, had a troubled past. Beginning in the mid-1960s outside the nearby town of Louden, outlaw bikers took over a hill behind the old Bryar Motor Sports Park. It became known as Animal Hill.

Today, New Hampshire International Speedway hosts the Louden Classic. This race is part of the U.S. Superbike Series, which means Daytona's Gatorade set migrates north.

A milder version of Animal Hill still exists, but most rallygoers in and around Laconia are peaceful, law-abiding lifestyle bikers. All riders can enjoy a modest array of rally activities and the tree-lined roads of New Hampshire's lake district.

In HOG We Trust: A Kinder, Gentler Rally

Local chapters of the Harley Owners Group (HOG) and its affiliate, Ladies of Harley, host statewide and regional rallies and one giant national. HOG rallies are "cleaner," more family-oriented alternatives to hardcore events that are not sanctioned by the company. To enter, you must be a HOG member or an associate. "Hoggies" are easy to spot.

Besides the club colors (logo insignias), many members wear leather or denim vests laden with dozens of pins and patches commemorating every biker event they've attended.

The poker run is a highlight of many HOG (and other) rallies. In one type of poker run, riders pay an entrance fee to take a scenic ride. At checkpoints, they draw cards or chips. Prizes are based on the best poker hands, and proceeds from entrance fees are donated to charity. You can "Stud Your Duds" at a Ladies of Harley workshop or enter your bike in a ride-in show. All bikes, no matter how radically modified, must be ridden, not trailered, to the grounds. Most entries combine an elegant and costly mix of function and fantasy.

Now that Harley-Davidson has become an American institution, every five years, the company celebrates its anniversary by hosting a reunion or homecoming. June 1993 was Harley's ninetieth birthday. En route to the party in Milwaukee, about sixty-eight thousand motorcycles formed a thundering procession that stretched for thirty miles. The parade lasted over three hours—nothing but bikes as far as the eye could see. Thousands of spectators lined the route, giving the bikers high fives and waving American flags. Proceeds in excess of $1 million, collected from admissions to reunion events, were donated to the Muscular Dystrophy Association.

Hardcore Rallies: 1% of the Scene

At the opposite (low) end of the spectrum are the hardcore gatherings. These include the Easyriders Rodeos sponsored by the magazine of the same name. Similar events may have "American Motorcycle" or "Harley" in their titles, but they are *not* sanctioned by the Harley-Davidson Motor Company. You may be greeted at the gate by video cameramen urging you to "show your tits." The tattoo and wet T-shirt contests are the high culture here.

RALLIES FOR RIDERS OF ALL BIKES
Touring Rallies: Big-Bike Nations

There are many gatherings for riders of all brands. The touring rally is one such get-together. Americade, held each June in Lake George, New York, is the grandest of them all, drawing anywhere from twenty thousand to seventy-five thousand enthusiasts over the course of a week.

Touring riders who come to Americade include many older couples on behemoth, fully dressed touring rigs. "Full dressers" are powerful motorcycles equipped with so many amenities, they are akin to two-wheeled motor homes. The most popular of these is the Honda Gold Wing, seconded by similar rigs from the other Japanese manufacturers. BMW and Harley-Davidson have versions as well.

Touring couples are the Ozzie and Harriets of motorcycling. Typically, the husband steers the luxury vehicle while the wife sits back in a plush seat with armrests. Some couples wear matching outfits and helmets with intercoms and microphones. Many rear trunks are platforms for stuffed animals, while others are inscribed with the couples' names—Bob and Bitsy here, Hank and Hannah there.

Peeking out from among the rows of yachts-on-wheels are other types of bikes, especially those owned by sport riders who come to sample the curvy Adirondacks roads. The crowd is friendly but machines with

Courtesy Motor Maids

The Motor Maids at their 53d Annual Convention in 1993.

modified or unmuffled pipes are nearly booed out of town.

On the other hand, there is much applause for the full dresser light parade, where motorcycles are festooned with so many bulbs, they look like Disneyland floats. There are awards for the best-dressed couple, youngest and oldest riders, looniest license plate, and competitions for an Americade Queen and King. Anyone wearing too much leather—that is, anyone who looks too much like a "biker"—need not apply.

In short, Americade is a high-school prom for middle-aged "kids." Similar but smaller are the Rider Rallies sponsored by *Rider* magazine at sites around the country. Other (brand-specific) touring rallies include the Honda Hoot, put on by the Honda Riders Club of America (HRCA), and the Wing Ding of the Gold Wing Road Riders Association (GWRRA).

Women's Rallies: Where "The Girls" Are

The three national women's clubs—Motor Maids, Women on Wheels, and Women in the Wind—hold annual rallies in different states. Women's rallies offer samplings of the usual social, competitive, and informational activities over three or four days, but the ambience at each gathering is as different as the clubs are from one another.

Of a Motor Maids convention, humorist Erma Bombeck once said, "It looked more like a midlife Tupperware party where 'the girls,' as they call themselves, sit around and spin stories."

Except that these are no ordinary "girls." These are members of the nation's oldest women's riding club, and the stories are about the many millions of miles that they, collectively, have ridden. The older members recall how motorcycling used to be, before the days of biker chic and outlaw bikers. Snippets of conversations overheard include:

"Did you ever think you'd be selling ladies' underwear in your Harley dealership?"

"Please don't call us meter maids or motorcycle mamas. You won't find any tattoos or halter tops here."

The Motor Maids hold their conventions in July. The first one in 1944 drew fourteen riders. Today, roughly two hundred of the club's five hundred members attend, but other than their numbers, not much has changed. A favorite contest is the decades-old

Vera Griffin Collection

Field games haven't changed much in half a century. Back in the 1940s, Helen Blansitt of St. Louis, Missouri, rode the plank, as rallygoers do today.

The Peterson family of Jacksonville, Illinois: three generations of motorcycle enthusiasts converge at a Women on Wheels Ride-In.

timed road run, in which riders navigate varying terrain and arrive at checkpoints within designated time slots. The traditional Motor Maids parade looks like a sea of blue, gray, and white. Behind their tall windshields are the blue shirts, gray slacks, white gloves, and white boots of their uniforms . . . and the gray and white hair of the many lifetime members. If it sounds quaint, consider this: Club rules state that all Motor Maids must *ride* their bikes to the convention—trailering, even for octogenarians traveling a thousand miles or more, is unthinkable.

Believe the husbands when they say it isn't easy being married to a Motor Maid. One man complained: "You can't tell the guys you rode a million miles and sound macho, because your wife is right next to you doing the same thing!"

Stroll the parking lot at a Women on Wheels Ride-In, and you might wonder if WOW should change its name to WAF, for Warm and Fuzzy. Like the true touring riders that they are, many WOW members have stuffed animals bungeed to their bikes. Others have unicorns, owls, and Disney characters airbrushed on gas tanks. Inside the host hotel are two hundred to three hundred women, many in their forties and fifties.

WOW leaders, from left, Kathy Heller, Susan Konopka, and Sue Frish accept the AMA Brighter Image Award from AMA trustee Patty Mills.

hood. If you ride a foreign bike, you're welcome to join the club, but be prepared for some friendly ribbing.

The Women in the Wind "uniform" is ride-as-you-are: cowboy boots and jeans, bandannas over braids, and why bother with makeup when you know your face will be a mess from riding? Vests sport the club colors—a caricature of a woman riding, wearing shades, her hair blown wild by the wind.

Every July, they gather at what appears to be a giant coffee klatch.

But with WOW as with the Motor Maids, appearances are deceiving. The woman next to you in the cotton blouse and slacks has just ridden solo from Alaska. The young mother with her toddlers and their grandmother are veteran riders from a multigenerational motorcycling family where no one stays home to mind the kids—because the kids come everywhere in the sidecar. Husbands, boyfriends, even a few fathers are such strong supporters that nominations are taken for a "Mr. WOW."

When Women in the Wind get together in late June for their Summer Nationals, the host campground and nearby motel rock with the laughter of one hundred fifty boisterous women, many of whom are Harley lifestyle bikers in their thirties and forties. Local chapters have names like Wild Bunch, Smokey Mountain Thunder, Southern Maidinz, Free Spirits, and Empowered Sister-

Lin Litousky rode down from Canada for a Women in the Wind Ladies Run at Sturgis. That's a painting of a scantily clad *man* on the gas tank of her bike, "Lady's Night."

**A future biker catches a few
winks at a sidecar rally.**

Some husbands and boyfriends, who look as though they could hold their own in any brawl, have enough sense of humor to allow themselves to be whooped and hollered into donning T-shirts that say "Property of Women in the Wind." Don't miss the male "best buns" and beard contests.

There is something electric and liberating at the women-only Mid-Atlantic Women's Motorcycle Rally. This annual June gathering in Maryland was started in the early 1990s and has gotten good reviews for the diversity of the attendees, and the open, laid-back atmosphere where women of all ethnic backgrounds and persuasions mingle comfortably. Without male partners around, everyone can "let it all hang out." One attendee, sharing her experience in *Women on Wheels* magazine, wrote, "I loved my walk on the (sorta) wild side. I felt free to indulge my fantasies and be rid of conservatism and the restrictions I place on myself in real life.' " Rally proceeds go to the Susan G. Komen Breast Cancer Foundation.

Rallies Geared to
Specific Bike Brands

BMW Motorcycle Owners of America (MOA) and the BMW Riders Association (RA) each host a national rally drawing several thousand devotees, and local chapters of both clubs host smaller gatherings.

BMW riders are campers known for their wry humor and "secret society" clannishness. The local rallies have names like Beer Hunter, Udder Nonsense, It's Hard to Be Humble, and the Rolling Broccoli Camp Out and Nude Line Dancing Party. Within the ranks are many upscale professionals who get eccentric at the rallies. Aficionados of BMW's signature engine, the "boxer," with its horizontal-twin cylinders, may wear boxer shorts over their pants.

Beemers are built for autobahns, not boulevard cruising. Very few have custom paint jobs, and chrome sightings are rare. Rallygoers will inspect your odometer because hard miles, not paint, is the stuff of which war stories are made. The most superior, or insane, of BMW devotees are the Iron Butts, who rig auxiliary fuel cells to their bikes and ride thousand-mile days just to win mileage contests and bragging rights.

There are rallies for just about every type of bike and rider, including exotic Moto Guzzis, long-defunct Indians, and British bikes. In Ohio, the AMA hosts Vintage Motorcycle Days, featuring a bike auction, vintage road racing, motordrome stunt riders, and more. At sidecar rallies, you'll see lots of parents with children and dogs, as well as seniors and some disabled adults who enjoy motorcycling with a third wheel.

According to *Blackriders* magazine, there are an estimated two hundred thousand African-American motorcycle owners in the country. In recent years, more and more are attending all types of rallies. There are also gatherings organized by, and geared to, black riders. The week-long National Round-Up is considered one of the best.

Charity Rides

Charities have long been beneficiaries of bikers' generosity. Some charity rides have turned into enormous events, with parades of bikes that stretch for miles. The larger events conclude with a barbecue and recreation, including concerts, bike shows, and door prizes. At some events, you pay a flat entry fee; for others, you must raise pledges or bring checks from sponsors.

In Glendale, California, the Harley-dominated Love Ride to benefit the Muscular Dystrophy Association has become perhaps the largest single-day motorcycle fund-raiser in the world, with more than twenty thousand riders raising upward of a million dollars a year. It helps that the list of VIP participants is a who's who of Hollywood's celebrity biker set. Jay Leno, along with Peter Fonda and Dennis Hopper, who starred in the cult film *Easy Rider,* are the grand marshals. Mary Hart of TV's *Entertainment Tonight* rides in the parade, as do actors Lorenzo Lamas, Larry Hagman, and others.

Honda's Ride for Kids, benefiting the Pediatric Brain Tumor Foundation of the United States, consists of a dozen rides in various states. Since their beginnings in 1984, the rides have raised more than $2.5 million. Bikers raise money for many other charities as well, ranging from the March of Dimes Birth Defects Foundation to the Make-a-Wish Foundation. Clubs hold bike washes and other events to benefit battered women's shelters and veterans' hospitals. For Christmas toy runs, riders turn out even in bone-chilling weather to deliver toys to children who are orphaned, troubled, or disabled.

In the week preceding each Memorial Day, tens of thousands of bikers from across the nation, including many Harley-riding Vietnam vets, join the Run to the Wall, a mass pilgrimage to Rolling Thunder in Washington, D.C. Rolling Thunder is a procession of bikes that begins at the Pentagon and ends with a subdued but emotionally charged visit to the Vietnam Memorial.

One-Day and Weekend Events

In most areas, there are plenty of one-day activities. The riding season may begin with a bike blessing, during which a priest sprinkles holy water on the bikes and riders.

Sunday is traditionally the day when local clubs host events like field meets, swap meets, poker runs, and observation runs (take a scenic ride, look for clues, win a door prize).

An annual rite of spring: the blessing of the bikes.

Gypsy tours, which date back to the mid-1920s, are longer group rides over one or two days; they usually end in an idyllic setting with a barbecue and recreation. Two-day, five-hundred-mile rides that cover challenging roads are popular. The most well known of these include the Ramapo 500 for street bikes in the New York tristate area, and the Ridgerunner 500 for dual-sport bikes in California. There are midnight runs and even polar bear runs in the winter.

Events are hosted by all types of specialty clubs. These include the Blue Knights, comprised of law enforcement personnel; the Red Knights, a group for firefighters; the Knights of Life, who are medical professionals; and the Retreads, who are over forty. There are meetings of the Christian Motorcyclist Association and of "clean and sober" groups for recovering alcoholics. There are clubs and events for just about everyone.

Cycle Watering Holes
Sometimes, rallies are where you make them. Unpretentious diners, dairy barns, and snack bars have a way of becoming biker landmarks if they're situated on or near great riding roads. These rest stops are Sunday-morning watering

holes where bikers pause to exchange stories and show off a bit before roaring off in small groups to partake of their favorite pastime. Three of the most famous spots are Marcus Dairy in Danbury, Connecticut; Alice's Restaurant in Woodside, northern California; and the Rock Store, a deli nestled in the mountains near Malibu, just west of Hollywood. Here, celebrity bikers mingle with the nonfamous. And if you think cruise nights are only for cars, think again. On summer nights, hot-dog joints with big parking lots have a way of filling up with bikes.

With such a full social calendar of annual rallies, runs, and hangouts all across the continent, newcomers to motorcycling may wonder how they could have missed all this activity before. When bikers get together, motorcycles are social lubricants, demographic levelers, and, ultimately, adhesives for cherished friendships.

CHAPTER TEN

Choosing the right motorcycle to suit your needs, level of experience, and riding style is a highly personal decision and not often a simple one. As motorcycles have become safer (better brakes, better tires), faster, and more comfortable than those our parents and grandparents rode, they have become more specialized. The major considerations that should influence your choice of a motorcycle are:

- Type or classification of the bike, including its handling characteristics
- Type of riding you intend to do most. Do you plan to: Commute in urban traffic? Take leisurely long-distance tours? Challenge yourself with fast, sporting rides on twisty paved roads? Explore dirt trails? All of the above?

OPPOSITE: BMW's R850 Roadster

(BMW of North America)

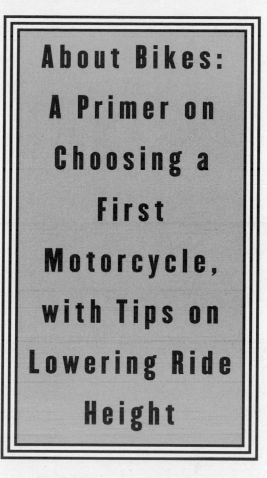

About Bikes: A Primer on Choosing a First Motorcycle, with Tips on Lowering Ride Height

- Ergonomics, including seat height and seating posture
- Weight, including center of mass or gravity (CG)
- Configuration and power output of the engine
- Style or aesthetic appeal

- Initial purchase price
- Subsequent costs in money *and* time for repairs and maintenance

While some motorcycles are as different from one another as sports cars are from station wagons, most bikes have this in common: They are designed for that half of the population who tend to be taller, heavier, and have more upper-body strength than the average female. Women who are taller or stronger than average and those with more advanced riding skills may not be concerned with some of the issues addressed here.

Motorcycles in the cruiser class are popular among women because they have low seats and a low CG. But short riders may not wish to be limited to one type of bike. What can they do? There are ways to lower many bikes, but first, let's look at what is available straight from the factories.

Because it would take a separate volume to cover all there is to say about bikes, we'll make certain *generalizations to summarize the hallmarks* of each category. Only types and brands of bikes widely available in North America are included. Some discontinued models are mentioned because they are excellent examples of their class and can be found used. Prices aren't listed because the range is too great. Five hundred bucks could get you a used, running wreck; thirty thousand would bring you a custom showpiece. We'll focus on street bikes, meaning motorcycles that are legal to ride on paved roads.

Today's street motorcycles are shifted manually (unlike automatic scooters). Most new models have hydraulic disc brakes, though some have a mechanical drum brake in the rear. A drum is not as efficient as a disc, but on some models, a rear drum is adequate because the front brake has 70 to 80 percent of the bike's stopping power, anyway. BMWs were the first motorcycles to come with antilock disc brakes (ABS); only a few models from other manufacturers have them.

A motorcycle is driven by a chain, belt, or shaft. A chain is the cheapest method, and it is light, efficient, and provides smooth gear shifts, but a chain must be lubricated and adjusted frequently. This can be a messy, annoying task. Belts and shafts are practically maintenance-free.

Street motorcycles have four-stroke internal combustion engines with one to six cylinders. Each cylinder has a piston. To complete one revolution, or "rev," of the motor's crankshaft, each piston makes four strokes. RPM means revolutions per minute. Engines may be cooled by air, oil, or water. When stuck in a summer traffic jam, a liquid-cooled engine is less prone to overheating than one cooled only by airflow. Engine size is measured by the volume in cubic centimeters (cc's) or cubic inches (ci's) of fuel/air mixture that is displaced by the pistons. Small or "entry level" street bike engines may displace anything from 125 to 450cc's. Midsized bikes fall roughly in the 500 to 850cc range. Large bikes blow out 900 to 1500cc's.

You'd think that the larger the displacement, the more horsepower. That's not always true. A four-cylinder, state-of-the-art 600cc sport bike may outrun a two-cylinder cruiser with twice the engine displacement. What happens when rubber meets road is determined by many factors, including:

- The number of cylinders
- How quickly and efficiently engine power is transmitted to the crankshaft
- The weight of the bike
- How aerodynamic the bike's outer bodywork is

A motorcycle's weight varies widely according to bike type, size, accessories, and other factors. Dry (without gas), an entry-level 175cc bike may weigh a mere 250 pounds, while a large cruiser or tourer can weigh 600 to 800 pounds. A full tank of gas, saddlebags, and windshields add pounds.

In many cases, total poundage is not the issue, but center of gravity is. You want to know where the machine carries most of its weight or mass. A cruiser carries most of it low, so a small person may handle the machine comfortably in most situations. But a touring bike, top-heavy with accessories and a full fairing (a large windscreen that protects the head, hands, and legs), might be unwieldy for a small person.

Lawrence Grodsky, who runs a rider training school in Pennsylvania and writes a safety column for *Rider* magazine, points out that the average female has roughly half the upper-body strength of the average male, and her inseam is generally two inches shorter. If she cannot plant both feet squarely on the ground, she must support more of the bike's weight at rest. According to Grodsky, "on a tall machine, the difference may exceed a hundred pounds."[1]

Generally, the best advice for most beginners is to start on a small or "smallish" bike.

Too much power in the hands of a novice who is just learning to operate the machine can be counterproductive. A not-uncommon scenario is one that occurs when a novice has a well-intentioned male partner who encourages her to start on a bike that is too tall, too top-heavy, or too powerful for her skill level. The result may cause a real dip in confidence.

Learn to ride *before* purchasing a motorcycle! Believe it or not, many people buy motorcycles without a clue as to how to ride them out of the dealership. Start by taking the Motorcycle RiderCourse, taught by the Motorcycle Safety Foundation (see Chapter 11 and the appendix for more information).

Once you've learned the basics, buy a used, inexpensive motorcycle. Make your mistakes on that machine. Observe what you like about the bike and what you don't. Then listen to yourself. With experience, you now have a reference point for choosing a suitable motorcycle. Keep in mind that in many cases, men's motorcycling needs *are* different. To a 180-pound man who carries a passenger, a 650cc bike may seem puny and underpowered. But for a 115-pound woman riding solo, a 650 may be quite adequate. Bikes are affected by power-to-weight ratio—how heavy the bike and rider(s) are will affect how powerful the bike "feels."

Following are the different types or categories of motorcycles. Bikes pictured are 1996 models except where noted.

SPORT BIKES: TWO-WHEELED ROCKETS

Sport bikes are designed for performance, not long-distance comfort. They have aerody-

Discover Today's Motorcycling

The discontinued Honda Hawk GT 650. Fully loaded, this midsized standard had plenty of power in its performance V-twin to carry the author (BELOW) around the continent during her working travels.

Becky Brown

namic plastic bodywork to help the bike punch a hole in the air with minimal wind drag. The handlebars are placed low and forward, while the footpegs are rearset. This forces you to crouch over the gas tank like a jockey. You support your weight primarily with your arms, wrists, and shoulders.

A sport bike has a short wheelbase (the distance between front and rear axles) and a steep rake. Basically, rake is the angle of the steering head (the front fork pivot, at the center of the handlebars) in relation to an imaginary vertical line. The shorter or steeper the rake angle, the closer the front axle is to the steering head, and the quicker the bike is to steer.

Sport bikes are generally chain-driven and they have powerful disc brakes and wide, sticky tires for maximum traction. They have high ground clearance to allow tremendous lean angles. This usually means two things: a seat height of thirty-one inches or more and a high center of gravity. In certain situations—like stopping on hills and pulling away from a stop on a sloped road—a large sport bike with a high seat and high mass may pose added challenges for a short rider. If both feet cannot reach the ground, you must slide to the left side of the seat and balance the bike using one leg as an outrigger. Since most women have good *lower*-body strength, this isn't a problem as long as the bike is straight up. If it starts to lean, you'll need a strong lower back, shoulders, pectorals, and arms to keep the bike up.

Many sport bikes have engines with an inline-four configuration, meaning four cylinders in line with the chassis. Inline-fours make their best power in the higher gears—when you're going fast. They can feel com-

paratively sluggish in stop-and-go traffic. Some modern sport bikes can rocket from zero to 150 and even up to 170 miles per hour right off the showroom floor. They are thrilling, but it is advisable to get some experience before you buy one. Street-legal sport bikes, when stripped of parts like lights and horns, become superbikes at the racetrack.

Midsized sport bikes include the Honda CBR 600, Kawasaki Ninja 600, Yamaha FZR 600, and Suzuki RF 600. Kawasaki's entry-level Ninjas, the 500 and 250R, have two cylinders instead of four.

CRUISERS: CHROME AND GLORY

Cruisers or "customs" are everything sport bikes are not. Cruisers have chromed parts and their owners tend to embellish them with accessories. Strip away the baubles and a cruiser is simplicity in motion. The engine is

Honda's CBR600F3, a quintessential sport bike with an inline four engine

American Honda Motor Company

1.

2.

An array of eye-catching cruisers:
1. Honda Rebel 250
2. Kawasaki Vulcan 500 LTD
3. Suzuki Savage 650
4. Yamaha Virago 750
5. Harley-Davidson Sportster 883 Hugger
6. Harley-Davidson Dyna Low Rider
7. Harley-Davidson Heritage Softail Classic

About half of all street bikes sold in 1995 were cruisers. Small cruisers are somewhat "forgiving" of a novice's clumsy techniques. It's advisable to have some experience before climbing aboard the larger bikes numbered 4 through 7.

3.

4.

5.

6.

7.

Kawasaki Motors Corp.

A luxury tourer, the Kawasaki Voyager XII

exposed and treated as part of the bike's overall styling.

Cruisers have high, curved, or "buckhorn" handlebars sloped back toward the rider. The footpegs are set forward. This places you in a leisurely, laid-back position for boulevard cruising or long-haul interstate trips. Cruisers, especially small to midsized models, are favored by short riders because of their modest seat heights. Cruisers' low center of gravity, long rake, and long wheelbase provide rock-solid straight-line stability but make them slower to handle on twisty roads. Yet speed is so irrelevant that some cruisers don't have a tachometer to indicate RPM. The essence of the ride is the feel of the V-twin engine.

In the minds of most people, there are basi-cally two types of cruisers: Harleys and the Japanese look-alikes. Harley's V-shaped, dual-cylinder, air-cooled engine, essentially unchanged since before World War II, has a deep, loud rumble and vibration that is overwhelming and powerful. Most foreign cruisers have refined versions of the V-twin engine that are usually liquid cooled and shaft driven. They rumble but the ride is smoother and easier on the bike. They require less maintenance.

Harleys are big-displacement machines. The "smallest" Harleys are the 883cc Sportster and the Hugger, a Sportster with a twenty-seven-inch seat height. Large Harley cruisers, or "Big Twins" (1340cc or 80ci), include the Heritage Softail Classic, Springer Softail, Fat Boy, and the Dyna Low Rider.

Cruisers have become so popular that three formerly discontinued, entry-level import models are back: Honda's Rebel 250; Yamaha's Virago 250 (formerly, the Route 66); and Suzuki's Savage 650. Kawasaki's Vulcan 500 LTD evokes the old 454 LTD. Midsized models include Suzuki's Intruder 800 and Honda's Shadow 600 and (four-cylinder) Magna 750. Discontinued entry-level cruisers that can be found used include Honda's Rebel 450, Shadow 500, and Magna 500. Not all of these models have a V-twin centerpiece, but all have that classic cruiser look.

TOURERS: ALL DRESSED UP

Tourers, a.k.a. full-dressers or rigs, are the Winnebagos of motorcycles, built for the long-distance comfort of driver and passenger. Touring bikes are huge, smooth, and powerful. Honda's new Gold Wing models have carlike, six-cylinder engines and a reverse gear. The dresser seating posture is upright, as in your favorite armchair.

There are so many options for full-luxury models that you can create your own rolling universe. Like cars, dressers have dashboards and sophisticated wiring systems to support amenities that may include anything from a CB radio, stereo, and tape deck to heated handgrips, blindingly bright headlights, and auxiliary lights. Fuel capacity is gargantuan, as is the luggage capacity of the built-in hard bags.

The downside is that dressers are top-heavy and their wide, plush saddles are beyond the reach of many short riders. These bikes glide on the interstate, but "flicking" one through twisty roads takes getting used to. Stopping all that mass requires careful attention to braking.

All of the manufacturers have dressers, which are great for experienced riders. The Kawasaki Voyager 1200 has a relatively low ride height of 29.7 inches. The adjustable seat on BMW's R1100RT goes down to 30.7 inches. Since both bikes are narrower than other tourers, they could work for some short riders.

SPORT-TOURERS: PERFORMANCE WITH SOME COMFORT

Sport-tourers are the "performance sedans" of motorcycles. These machines are hybrids for long-distance riders who want enough handling capabilities to make straying off the interstate fun, but don't confuse sport-touring with "dual-sport" or "adventure touring," as these bikes are not built for rough terrain. Sport-tourers are more passenger-friendly than true sport bikes, and many models come with integrated, removable hard luggage systems. Others carry soft luggage beautifully.

The innards and aerodynamic bodywork on the sportier models are descended from sport bikes. They have a relatively forward seating posture, relatively low, short handlebars, and a modest rake, all of which make them nimble enough for twisty roads, yet spare the rider from the cramped extremes of a true sport bike. Since most of these hybrids have a wholesome fuel capacity and high ground clearance, they tend to be tall and have a high center of gravity.

The designation itself—sport-tourer—is an oxymoron and a hint of compromise. If a sport-tourer has wind protection, it is usually an aerodynamic, frame-mounted fairing or

Yamaha Motor Corp.

Yamaha's Seca II 600 is a nimble, midsized sport-tourer that's fun to ride.

half-fairing that protects the torso and shoulders. Your helmet remains in the breeze and this can make or break the ride. If you're going slow enough or riding on narrow roads where trees block the wind, you'll be fine, but if you're droning on a windy interstate for hundreds of miles, you may experience heights of fatigue and discomfort that you never thought possible from a motorcycle.

The aerodynamic fairing/windshield is supposed to deflect the wind blast over your helmet to place your head in a pocket of "dead air." If you were tucked down as on a superbike, this would work. But you're touring, not racing. The slope, width, and height of the shield, the angle and height of the handlebars, the length of your arms and torso, may all conspire to place your head in a line

of turbulence. At interstate speeds, your head can bob like a dashboard doll. Your neck muscles may cramp as you attempt to hold your head level. The wind roar can be so loud, your ears may ring long after you're off the bike. Some full-face helmets and earplugs can lessen, but not prevent, the problem. Certain sport-touring windshields are adjustable, but often not enough to make a big difference. Aftermarket (nonfactory) designers have a variety of windshields and peripheral attachments to redirect the turbulence.

Despite the compromises, many riders love sport-tourers for their fine handling and versatility, but the pickings for entry-level and even midsized models are slim. There are Honda's Pacific Coast 800 and the Yamaha Seca II 600. The adjustable seat on BMW's

R1100RS makes it lower than other bikes of comparable engine displacement, but the bike is still massive.

STANDARD OR RETRO BIKES DO IT ALL

Standard motorcycles are all-around workhorses that harken back to what motorcycles were before they became specialized. Some models look like older bikes, hence the "retro" label. They are also known as "naked" bikes because typically they have minimal bodywork that leaves the engine exposed. They can be elegant or nondescript in their simplicity.

Standards don't accelerate or handle as quickly as sport bikes and they don't turn heads like cruisers. They don't offer the plush comfort of dressers and they're not overly happy on dirt roads. What they do is a little of everything, and they do it just fine. The seating posture is upright, sometimes slightly forward. There are many windshields for these bikes, so turbulence should not be a permanent problem. Standards tend to be tallish, with seats hovering at thirty inches or more.

A good standard is like a faithful dog—it's reliable and will come with you everywhere. Midsized models include the Honda Nighthawk 750 and Suzuki's Bandit 600 and GS500ET. BMW's R1100 and R850 Roadsters have adjustable seats and a lower CG than many standards in this displacement range. Entry-level standards include the Honda Nighthawk 250 and Suzuki GN125ET. Good

American Suzuki Motor Corp.

Suzuki's standard Bandit 600 is another nimble handler that's fun in the short haul. The Bandit, like the Seca II and Hawk GT, has a relatively forward seating posture that can feel cramped after a while.

American Suzuki Motor Corp.

Suzuki's DR125SET, an entry-level dual-sport

discontinued models are Kawasaki's 750 and 550 Zephyrs, the Suzuki Bandit 400, and the Honda Hawk GT 650 (different from the Nighthawk).

DUAL-SPORT OR ON/OFF-ROAD BIKES

Dual-sport, a.k.a. dual-purpose, motorcycles double as rugged street commuters and "adventure touring" bikes that can take you over hill, dale, and dirt. Most are light and narrow but very tall—seat heights tend to start around thirty-three inches. A high center of mass, long-travel suspension, and lots of ground clearance get these bikes over ruts and rocks. If you can manage the height, they are a hoot. Their resilient suspension may feel a bit wobbly on asphalt, but once you get used to it, you'll find them very maneuverable for skitting around urban traffic.

Most Japanese dual-sport bikes are small to midsized "thumpers" (single-cylindered). They are chain-driven and kick- or electric-started. Entry-level models include the Yamaha Serow 225 and Suzuki's DR 350, 200, and 125 SETs. The 125 is a relative midget with a narrow, 31.5-inch seat. If you're heavy enough, sometimes merely sitting on the smaller bikes lowers the suspension by a couple of inches.

OFF-ROAD OR DIRT-ONLY BIKES

Dirt bikes are built for off-road use only. They are lighter than dual-sports, and have high seats and lots of ground clearance for trail riding, motocross, and enduro competition. Dirt bikes for children come as small as 50cc so that kids old enough to ride bicycles can compete in "peewee" motocross races. Kawasaki's KX models in 125 and 80cc are popular among female motocrossers.

LOWERING A STREET BIKE TO FIT YOU

Sometimes, especially for short riders, the ideal street bike doesn't exist from the factory. Enter the aftermarket and the world of customization. Many bikes can be lowered by installing a lower seat, lower profile tires, a shorter rear shock absorber, and by adjusting the front suspension. With a combination of steps, ride height may be lowered by a couple of inches. These are fairly routine modifica-

tions that many repair shops do—but be aware that as soon as a bike is modified from its factory specifications, you may void your warranty. Some dealers will not modify bikes due to liability concerns. This section is *not* intended as a do-it-yourself guide, nor as a substitute for consultation with a trained mechanic.

Lowering modifications must be done carefully. If the motorcycle's rear end is lowered more than a tad, the bike's steering geometry is altered and its handling may be compromised. Your mechanic must adjust the front suspension proportionately. On some bikes, this is done by raising the fork tubes in the triple-clamps (for simplicity's sake, this is a minor adjustment that lowers the front

Kawasaki Motors Corp.

The Kawasaki KX 80, a favorite among young motocrossers

end). Sometimes, different fork springs are also needed. Not all bikes are built with leeway for such alterations.

Research tires carefully. A lower-profile tire means a wider tire. Will it fit the rim and clear the wheel supports? Call the tire manufacturers. Their customer service reps will tell you if they make a tire to fit your bike, though at the same time, they will not go on record as *recommending* anything other than the OEM (original equipment manufactured) tire that came with the bike.

Lowering a motorcycle may cost some ground clearance. It will be harder to lift the bike onto its centerstand. The angle of the sidestand will be steeper, which means the bike will lean less when parked. You may need to have the sidestand shortened and welded by a professional. As for the seat, sometimes shaving off a bit of foam from the top and sides can make the difference. If this proves uncomfortable, turn to the aftermarket seat companies.

If you have your heart set on a certain bike, the compromises may be worth the initial outlay of cash and time, but before you have any modifications done, talk to several dealers

and mechanics. Hang around the shop and talk to other riders, especially riders of the same model. Find out if there is a club or owners network devoted to your particular bike or marque—newsletters are great for word-of-mouth information.

The motorcycle magazines are excellent sources from which to learn about bike anatomy, parts, accessories, and all kinds of customizations. Most topics are perennials—pick up several magazines in any month, and you may find an article (and surely plenty of ads) about the subject you're researching, whether it's the right seat, the right motor oil—or the right new or used bike. A highly informative, easily readable textbook is *Motorcycles: Fundamentals, Service, Repair* by Bruce Johns and David Edmundson (Goodheart-Willcox, 1987). For details on specific new and out-of-production models, check out Ian Smith's Motorcycle Reports and bound volumes of *Cycle World* road tests. See the Riders' Resource Directory (page 178) for addresses of manufacturers and distributors of motorcycles, parts, and accessories, as well as sources for more information.

Triumph USA

Triumph motorcycles made a comeback in recent years. This 885cc Thunderbird recalls British "cafe racers" of the fifties and sixties. The Rockers (rivals of the Mods—remember them?) hung out at London's Ace Cafe and held impromptu drag races. Comic-book biker Barb Wire rides a T-bird on film.

BMW of North America

And They Said It Couldn't Be Done . . .

The BMW K75RT is a discontinued midsized touring bike with a loyal ridership. BMW's low-seat kit brings the saddle down to 29.9 inches, but since the bike is as wide as a hippopotamus, it is still quite a reach. A Progressive Suspension short shock and low-profile Metzeler street radial tires brought the ride height down dramatically on the author's K75RT. The front fork tubes were raised in the triple clamps; this shortened the steering rake, making the bike slightly more responsive, or quicker to steer, in corners. The Metzeler radials improved traction. Although the shorter shock didn't always absorb bumps as well, and the side-stand and centerstand had to be shortened, in some ways the lowered bike was a better bike.

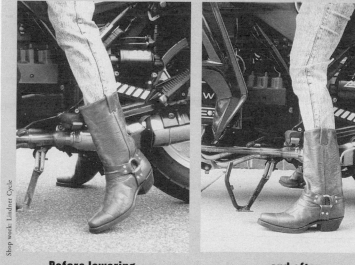

Shop work: Lindner Cycle

Before lowering . . .   . . . and after

It's midnight when a sudden downpour takes you by surprise...

Do you know what to do? Take the *Motorcycle RiderCourse*®.

Motorcycle Safety Foundation

Motorcycling is often described as a healthy risk-taking activity. And it is—as long as you have a healthy awareness of the fact that the risks are real and that they apply to you, too.

Basic Motorcycle Safety and Risk Management, with Tips on Choosing Protective Gear

The Motorcycle Safety Foundation (MSF) runs a nationwide program of excellent rider training courses. According to the MSF, mile for mile, riding a motorcycle is sixteen times more likely to result in a fatality than driving a car. But that is a "blanket" statistic that doesn't reveal age, gender, or cause. The MSF says the two major factors that determine who gets in accidents are age and experience. The older you are and the more riding experience you have, the less likely you are to have an accident. Traffic safety expert James McNight was once quoted as saying, "Males crash because of testosterone, females from inexperience." The first six months of riding are when mishaps are most likely.

In 1981, a comprehensive study of nine hundred motorcycle accidents in the Los Angeles area was published by the University of Southern California Traffic Safety Center. Commonly called the Hurt Study (after head researcher Dr. Harry Hurt), the report is still considered a landmark.[1]

The findings revealed that three-fourths of motorcycle accidents involved collision with a car, and two-thirds of these accidents were caused when the car violated the motorcycle's right-of-way, mostly by turning left in front of the oncoming bike at an intersection. The most common excuse car drivers gave was, basically, "Officer, I didn't see the motorcycle."

Hurt noted that typically, the rider had less than two seconds to take evasive action, adding, "The ability to countersteer and swerve was essentially absent." Many riders overbraked and skidded the rear wheel and underbraked the front. (The front brake has 70 to 80 percent of a bike's stopping power.)

Almost half of the fatalities in the study involved alcohol. Operating a motorcycle requires three to five times more coordination skills than driving a car. The MSF points out that, theoretically, the same amount of alcohol that might not be a problem for a person driving a car could make a lethal difference to the same person when riding a motorcycle. (This does *not* mean it is okay to drink alcohol and operate a car!)

HOW TO MANAGE THE RISKS

Covering every principle of motorcycle safety is beyond the scope of this book, but there are several important areas that the MSF and other safety groups emphasize. Here are some guidelines. *Guidelines are not intended as a substitute for a safety course.* Phone numbers and addresses for all the resources and products mentioned are in the appendix.

Take a Rider Training Course

The Hurt Study found that rider training reduced accident involvement and was related to reduced injuries. Since the time the study was conducted, motorcycle fatalities have declined by nearly half.[2] Rider training is often cited as a major reason.

MSF courses are taught at more than seven hundred sites around the country. To find a site near you, call 800-446-9227. Novices use demo bikes provided by the MSF. If you have at least three months of experience, you are ready for the MSF's Experienced RiderCourse (ERC), for which you use your own bike.

Those with more advanced skills might consider California's Leading Advanced Safety School (CLASS), which travels to racetracks around the country. It is geared toward improving your riding *performance,* with emphasis on smoothness. As you get smoother, you get faster. You will come away with valuable skills that are applicable to the street.

Practice Evasive Maneuvers and Emergency Braking, and Be Alert to Predict Hazards

Riding a motorcycle as safely as possible requires a combination of defensiveness and "aggression" (for lack of a better word). Hurt noted that "lack of attention to the riding task is a common factor for the motorcyclist in an accident." You must always be alert and constantly predict potential traffic hazards. When riding, you make hundreds of decisions per mile. Be wary of those ubiquitous left-turning cars and slow down at intersections. It's common sense, but some riders, figuring they have the right-of-way, do not slow down enough. There's a saying: "You can be right or dead right."

As for "aggression," your bike is much more maneuverable than a car, and therefore you are better able to speed up, if appropriate, or swerve quickly to get out of the way of a hazard. A motorcycle does not steer according to the same principles as a four-wheeled vehicle. When swerving or turning, a bike leans, and so you must understand and use the technique of "countersteering."

Your motorcycle can stop quicker than the car or truck behind you—watch those rearview mirrors. Motorcycle brakes are powerful and must be applied properly. Chomping abruptly on the front brake, for instance, can cause your front wheel to lock, which would put you on the pavement immediately. In an emergency, though, you need all the stopping power you can get. Learn the art of what some call "threshold braking"—braking smoothly, firmly, but progressively.

Too much rear brake can cause a rear-wheel skid, which could also put you down if the motorcycle isn't moving in a straight line. Braking on wet pavement or gravel, in a curve, or when riding downhill require caution. The MSF has practice drills for these situations and others. As with martial arts, tennis, or anything else that requires mental and manual dexterity, these skills must be practiced to be perfected. You want to be so good at them that in an emergency, you'd do them automatically.

Every time you start the bike, psyche yourself up to concentrate on what you're about to do. Hurt found that most accidents happen close to home. Expect the unexpected. Think of every ride as a practice session and an opportunity to improve. This is part of the fun and challenge of riding. Exercise your mind by playing "what if" games. Having escape routes in mind could save your life.

Ride Within Your Limits

One-fourth of motorcycle accidents in the Hurt Study were single-vehicle mishaps. Of these, rider error was the major cause two-thirds of the time. The typical error was a slide-out and fall due to overbraking or running wide on a curve due to excess speed or undercornering. Ride with a margin for error. Knowing your limits also means getting off the bike if you're fatigued.

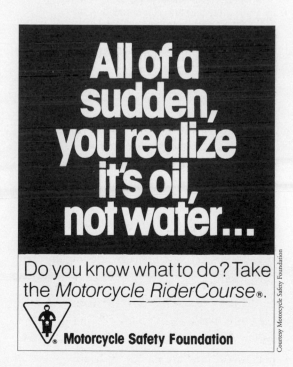

All of a sudden, you realize it's oil, not water...

Do you know what to do? Take the *Motorcycle RiderCourse*®.

Motorcycle Safety Foundation

Courtesy Motorcycle Safety Foundation

PUT YOUR
VALUABLES
IN A
SAFE PLACE.

Helmets make riding more comfortable and fun. Not to mention safer. Protect your most valuable asset. Always wear a helmet.
MOTORCYCLE SAFETY FOUNDATION

Courtesy Motorcycle Safety Foundation

Increase Your Visibility to Other Motorists

Hurt found that riders who made themselves conspicuous by wearing high-visibility yellow, orange, or bright red jackets were less likely to get hit. If you don't want to give up your black leather jacket, consider a removable, over-the-jacket vest made by a company that calls itself Conspicuity. The vests are made of a sheer, netted material that is available in black; brightly colored stripes are sewn on the netted material. The stripes are either fluorescent (for daytime visibility) or reflective (for nighttime). A light-colored helmet is preferable to a dark one. At the very least, put reflective stickers on your helmet. There is a removable band called a Halo that fits around the bottom of a full-face helmet. The Halo bands are either fluorescent or reflective.

Proper lane positioning is necessary to promote visibility. Ride in that portion of the lane that puts you in the best spot to scan the road and predict hazards, and also to be seen by others. Don't tailgate and don't ride in people's blind spots.

Wear Protective Gear

According to Hurt, the most deadly injuries were to the chest and head. A helmet was the single critical factor in the prevention of head injuries. At the least, Hurt recommended a helmet that was DOT approved; better still was a helmet approved by the Snell Foundation. Full-facial coverage helmets offered the most protection.

Not every injury is to the head, of course, and that is why it is advisable to wear a full set of protective gear. Besides a helmet, that would include a leather jacket, leather pants or chaps, boots or shoes above the ankle, leather gloves, and eye protection. If this sounds awfully stuffy for hot weather, it is, but there's another saying: "Better rawhide than your hide." Heavy-grade leather can withstand about a hundred feet of sliding on pavement before it will wear through. Cotton denim will be in tatters in just five or ten feet. Nylon can actually melt from the friction of a slide. All-season garments made of Kevlar, a highly abrasion-resistant fabric, are an alternative to leather.

There are also vented leather and Kevlar jackets with zippered areas that open to reveal a lining with airholes. These vented jackets do work, even in summer, except if you're stopped in traffic. In hot weather, you can sometimes stay *cooler* wearing a vented jacket over a wet shirt. Motorcyclists who live in desert climes sometimes wear several water-soaked layers and peel them off as they dry.

Women's motorcycle apparel has become all the rage, but designer leather duds are for disco dancing, not riding. Designer jackets and pants are made of softer, thinner leather, they are sewn with less sturdy stitching, and they lack certain features you'd want on the road. A real motorcycle jacket should have a wind flap behind the main zipper, zippered pockets, and zippered wrists to keep the wind from blowing up the sleeves. To accommodate the riding position, the jacket should also have longer sleeves, a longer waist in the back, and room at the shoulders. Roomy shouldn't mean loose or "blousy," as many women's jackets are. If the jacket is blousy, the wind will get in and cause the jacket to balloon. A loose jacket could also ride up in the event of a slide, exposing you to the pavement.

A few manufacturers of genuine motorcycle gear offer jackets in women's sizes, but be aware that some women's jackets aren't as functional as men's. The sleeves and waists are too short, they don't have as many (sometimes, not any) zippered compartments, and they may be sorely lacking in other basics. If you're willing to spend the bucks, some companies will custom-tailor garments for you.

In cool weather, look for gauntlet gloves, which have long, wide cuffs that extend over

Courtesy Harley-Davidson MotorClothes

Sturdy boots, such as these from Harley-Davidson MotorClothes, protect the ankles and shins. Boots can also shield the legs from excessive engine and exhaust heat.

your jacket wrists to keep the wind out. Designer gloves are better than nothing, but real motorcycle gloves are thicker; some have an extra layer of leather or padding on the palms.

Be Ready to Battle the Elements

One of the great joys—and potential health hazards—of riding a motorcycle is being exposed to the elements. On long trips especially, prepare for changes in the weather. Carry rain gear and extra layers.

Copyright © Femmegear

Dee Modglin, ABOVE, president of Femmegear in San Francisco, custom-tailors leather garments for women and is attentive to the needs of full-figured riders. According to Modglin, leathers for street riding should be at least 1.1 millimeters thick; sturdy, drum-dyed cowhide or buffalo hide are best. Femmegear selections are shown at LEFT. Seated on the bike, RIGHT, is motojournalist Jamie Elvidge, who road tests gear for *Motorcyclist* magazine.

In the warm months, take steps to prevent dehydration, heat fatigue, and heat stroke. As mentioned in the section on protective gear, sometimes covering up can be more comfortable than leaving your skin exposed to the hot sun. In any case, carry sunblock and water. You might also want to try a neckerchief called a Kool Tie. The Kool Tie is filled with absorbent granules, which, when soaked in water, expand and retain moisture. Unlike a conventional bandanna that dries in minutes from a warm wind, the Kool Tie may stay moist for days.

Dehydration can also occur in the cool months, as can hypothermia and frostbite. At rest stops, get inside, move around, stretch your limbs, and stay away from caffeine and nicotine. Caffeine is a diuretic that can rob your body of liquids. Caffeine and nicotine constrict capillaries and can leave your extremities more vulnerable to frostbite. Keep in mind that when you're riding, especially on an unfaired or minimally shielded bike, the windchill factor is much colder than what you hear on the weather report.

Your leather jacket is a windbreaker, but it is not warm in itself. You need to layer up beneath it. Start with underwear made of silk or a synthetic sweat-wicking fabric such as polypropylene. Real wool, which traps air and thus body heat, is best for subsequent layers. "Heated" vests, gloves, and even jackets and chaps are also available. These garments use your bike's battery power to heat up and stay toasty. Your rain jacket can double as a windbreaker. Worn *under* your leather jacket, it will really hold your body heat.

Prepare for the Unexpected

Carry these items:

- A first-aid kit. There are many compact kits available. Two geared toward motorcyclists are Adventure Medical Kits' Day Tripper and Pro-Light Cyclist. If you are allergic to any medications or have any conditions that medics should know about, carry the appropriate identification.

- Earplugs. On a long trip, you'll be glad you have them.

- Your bike's owner's manual and a tool kit for emergency repairs. New motorcycles come with tool kits. If your bike doesn't have one, the owner manual will tell you which tools to get. Supplement the kit with a small vise grip (handy for a broken clutch cable), electrical tape (handy for a hundred potential things), spare fuses, spark plugs, spare bulbs for headlight and brake light, a flashlight, a chain master-link if your bike has a chain, and a tire patch kit or spray can of compressed air and tire sealant. If your bike drinks a lot of oil, carry at least enough to "top off" until you get to a repair shop.

Maintain Your Bike and Inspect It Before Riding

Today's motorcycles are generally so reliable, many riders neglect the obvious. Keep your

The Harley-Davidson Enthusiast

Tuning Up

July, 1921

bike well maintained by following the service schedule in the owner's manual. Something as simple as a clogged fuel filter can put you on the side of the road. Change the oil, and if your bike doesn't have a "maintenance-free" battery, be sure to check the electrolyte level. Learn how your bike works. An unfamiliar rattling or "ratchety" noise can stem from something as basic as a loose chain.

If your bike feels wobbly, especially in a curve, pull over and check your tires. Underinflated tires are the most common cause of handling problems. The Motopump is a very compact pump and CO_2 cartridge kit that is handy to top off an underinflated tire. A flat tire, needless to say, would cause a *major* handling problem. A blowout can cause you to fall, so inspect your tires for nails and cracks before you set out. Also check the adjustment on your shock absorber; if your suspension isn't properly adjusted, the bike may feel unstable in corners.

T-CLOCK is an MSF acronym to remind you of what to check in your pre-ride inspection.

T: Tires and wheels
C: Controls (cables, hoses, throttle)
L: Lights (battery, lenses, reflectors, wiring, headlamp)
O: Oil (levels, leaks)
C: Chassis (frame, suspension, chain or belt, fasteners)
K: Kickstand (centerstand, sidestand)

The MSF has compiled a handbook called *Motorcycling Excellence: Skills, Knowledge and Strategies for Riding Right* (Boston: Whitehouse Press, 1995), which details the T-CLOCK routine, along with many other areas indicated in the book's title. It even has tips on lifting a fallen bike.

A Twist of the Wrist, a book and video set by road racing guru Keith Code, is geared to improving performance on the track, but Code has some excellent advice on concentration and the art of using visual reference points to get you safely (and quickly) through a curve. *Street Smarts* is a useful, multipart video and book for street riders. The motorcycle magazines have lots of articles on riding skills. Two of the best monthly columns are David Hough's nuts-and-bolts "Proficient Motorcycling" in *Motorcycle Consumer News* and Lawrence Grodsky's thought-provoking "Stayin' Safe" in *Rider.*

Trail, dirt, or off-road riding requires a different set of skills, a different type of bike and protective gear. The MSF book has a good section on off-road riding. Incidentally, learning to ride in the dirt can help your street skills.

A WORD ON GROUP RIDING

It is tempting for new riders, eager to be accepted in their local motorcycle community, to want to ride with a group. If you are unfamiliar with a particular group's riding style, don't "ride someone else's ride." If you are not comfortable with the group's pace, slow down. Ask the leader or road captain to establish a plan. Many groups allow for different skill levels. Faster riders go at their pace and wait at crossroads for slower ones. In this manner, everyone can enjoy the ride safely.

WHO YA GONNA CALL?

If traveling alone for any distance, consider carrying a cellular phone. Subscribe to an emergency roadside towing service geared to motorcyclists. One of the best is Motorcycle Towing Service (MTS), which offers a variety of benefits, including cellular phone rental, an emergency cash loan, and a guarantee that the proper equipment will be used to tow your bike. The American Motorcyclist Association and some of the large, nation-wide motorcycle clubs have emergency "help" networks. BMW Motorcycle Owners of America (BMWMOA), BMW Riders Association (BMWRA), Gold Wing Road Riders Association (GWRRA), and Harley Owners Group (HOG) are among such clubs.

As in any sport or endeavor that involves risks, the risks of motorcycling can be, and are, managed and minimized by responsible riders. With proper training, practice, and common sense, you can master the challenge and experience the joy of safe cycling.

Give Your Bike a "Brake"

This beautiful shovelhead Sportster, so nicknamed for the shape of its cylinder heads, is nearly twenty years old but wears its age well. Preventive maintenance is especially important on older bikes and those with high mileage. Brakes are among the most often neglected vital systems. Most bikes from the early seventies have a hydraulic disc brake in the front and a mechanical drum brake in the rear. To get the most power out of the front brake (or brakes, if there is a double disc), inspect and top off the fluid in the

master cylinder on a regular basis. Change the fluid at the service intervals in your owner's manual. Check brake pads for wear and change pads accordingly, and inspect calipers and hoses for leaks. Drum brakes must be adjusted periodically and worn linings must be replaced. Dirt and rust inside the drum can also hinder the mechanism. Overall, keeping a bike clean is the first step in maintaining it. When lubricating or cleaning, keep slippery substances off brake parts and tires.

T-CLOCK INSPECTION

T-CLOCK ITEM	WHAT TO CHECK	WHAT TO LOOK FOR	CHECK-OFF	
T—TIRES & WHEELS				
Tires	Condition	Tread depth, wear, weathering, evenly seated, bulges, imbedded objects.	Front	Rear
	Air Pressure	Check when cold, adjust to load/speed.	Front	Rear
Wheels	Spokes	Bent, broken, missing, tension, check at top of wheel "ring" okay—"thud," loose spoke.	Front	Rear
	Cast	Cracks, dents.	Front	Rear
	Rims	Out of round/true = 5mm. Spin wheel, index against stationary pointer.	Front	Rear
	Bearings	Grab top and bottom of tire and flex: No freeplay (click) between hub and axle, no growl when spinning.	Front	Rear
	Seals	Cracked, cut or torn, excessive grease on outside, reddish brown around outside.	Front	Rear
C—CONTROLS				
Levers	Condition	Broken, bent, cracked, mounts, tight, ball ends on handlebar lever.	Front	Rear
	Pivots	Lubricated.		
Cables	Condition	Fraying, kinks, lubrication: ends and length.		
	Routing	No interference or pulling at steering head, suspension, no sharp angles, wire looms in place.		
Hoses	Condition	Cuts, cracks, leaks, bulges, chafing, deterioration.		
	Routing	No interference or pulling at steering head, suspension, no sharp angles, wire looms in place.		
Throttle	Operation	Moves freely, snaps closed, no revving.		
L—LIGHTS				
Battery	Condition	Terminals, clean and tight, electrolyte level, held down securely.		
	Vent Tube	Not kinked, routed properly, not plugged.		
Lenses	Condition	Cracked, broken, securely mounted, excessive condensation.		
Reflectors	Condition	Cracked, broken, securely mounted.		
Wiring	Condition	Fraying, chafing, insulation.		
	Routing	Pinched, no interference or pulling at steering head or suspension, wire looms and ties in place, connectors tight, clean.		
Headlamp	Condition	Cracks, reflector, mounting and adjustment system.		
	Aim	Height and right/left.		

O—OIL

Levels	Engine Oil	Check warm or centerstand, dipstick, sight glass.		
	Hypoid Gear Oil	Transmission, rear driver, shaft.		
	Hydraulic Fluid	Brakes, clutch, reservoir or sight glass.		
	Coolant	Reservoir and/or coolant recovery tank—cool only.		
	Fuel	Tank or gauge.		
Leaks	Engine Oil	Gaskets, housings, seals.		
	Hypoid Gear	Gaskets, seals, breathers.		
	Hydraulic Fluid	Hoses, master cylinders, calipers.		
	Coolant	Radiator, hoses, tanks, fittings, pipes.		
	Fuel	Lines, fuel taps, carbs.		

C—CHASSIS

Frame	Condition	Cracks at gussets, accessory mounts, look for paint lifting.		
	Steering-Head Bearings	No detent or tight spots through full travel, raise front wheel, check for play by pulling/pushing forks.		
	Swingarm Bushings/ Bearings	Raise rear wheel, check for play by pushing/pulling swingarm.		
Suspension	Forks	Smooth travel, equal air pressure/damping antidive settings.	Left	Right
	Shock(s)	Smooth travel, equal preload/air pressure/damping settings, linkage moves freely and is lubricated.	Left	Right
Chain or Belt	Tension	Check at tightest point.		
	Lubrication	Side plates when hot. *Note:* Do not lubricate belts.		
	Sprockets	Teeth not hooked, securely mounted.		
Fasteners	Threaded	Tight, missing bolts, nuts.		
	Clips	Broken, missing.		
	Cotter Pins	Broken, missing.		

K—KICKSTAND

Centerstand	Condition	Cracks, bent.	
	Retention	Springs in place, tension to hold position.	
Sidestand	Condition	Cracks, bent (safety cut-out switch or pad if equipped).	
	Retention	Springs in place, tension to hold position.	

RIDERS' RESOURCE DIRECTORY

CONTENTS

ACCESSORIES, PARTS, RIDER GEAR

Accessories—General

Adventure Motorcycle Gear
P.O. Box 366
Springfield, VA 22150
800-217-3526
www.adventuremotogear.
  com

Chaparral Motorsports
555 H St.
San Bernardino, CA 92410
800-841-2960
www.chaparral-racing.com

Competition Accessories
345 W. Leffel Ln.
Springfield, OH 45506
800-543-8208
www.compacc.com

Dennis Kirk
955 South Field Ave.
Rush City, MN 55069
800-328-9280
www.denniskirk.com

J.C. Whitney
1 J.C. Whitney Way
P.O. Box 1000-0100
LaSalle, IL 61301
312-431-6102
www.jcwhitney.com

Lockhart-Phillips USA
P.O. Box 4802
San Clemente, CA 92672
800-221-7291
www.lockhartphillips.com

Motorcycle Accessory
  Warehouse
3620 Jeannine Dr.
Colorado Springs, CO 80917
800-241-2222
www.mawonline.com

Targa Accessories
21 Journey
Aliso Viejo, CA 92656
800-521-7945
www.targa-acc.com

Accessories—Brand-Specific

For BMWs

Bob's BMW
10720 Guilford Rd.
Jessup, MD 20794
301-497-8949
800-BMW-BOBS
www.bmwbobs.com

Capital Eurosport
45449 Severn Unit 179
Sterling, VA 20166
703-421-7860
800-642-5100 (USA)
800-445-4175 (CAN)

For British Bikes

British Cycle Supply, Ltd.
P.O. Box 119
Wolfville, NS B0P 1X0
CANADA
902-542-7478
www.canadianbiker.com/
britcycle.html

British Only
32341 Park Ln.
Garden City, MI 48135
734-421-0303
www.british-only.com

For Ducatis

Motofixx
505 N. Main St.
Port Chester, NY 10573
800-448-9363
www.motofixx.com

For Harleys

Arlen Ness
16520 E. 14 St.
San Leandro, CA 94578
510-276-3395
www.arlenness.com

Accessories—Brand-Specific (Cont'd)

Custom Chrome (CCI)
16100 Jacqueline Ct.
Morgan Hill, CA 95037
800-729-3332
www.customchrome.com

Drag Specialties
P.O. Box 9336
Minneapolis, MN 55440
800-222-3400
www.dragspecialties.com

Harley-Davidson Genuine
  Parts & Accessories
3700 W. Juneau Ave.
P.O. Box 653
Milwaukee, WI 53208
800-443-2153
www.harley-davidson.com

J & P Cycles
P.O. Box 138
Anamosa, IA 52205-0138
888-994-7677 (USA)
800-944-2201 (CAN)
www.j-pcycles.com

For Moto Guzzis

Harper's Moto Guzzi
32401 Stringtown Rd.
Greenwood, MO 64034
800-752-9735
www.harpermotoguzzi.com

For MX and Off-Road Bikes

Acerbis Plastica USA
13200 Greg St.
Poway, CA 92064
www.acerbis.com

APPAREL FOR RIDING

Apparel—Women's

Femmegear/MC Gear
5214-F Diamond Heights
  Blvd. Ste. 623
San Francisco, CA 94131
415-826-3598
info@femmegear.com
info@mcgear.com
www.femmegear.com
www.mcgear.com

GirlGear
176 East Saginaw Hwy.
Grand Ledge, MI 48837
517-627-8226
www.girlmotorcycle.com
Motocross apparel.

LadyRidersWear
P.O. Box 366
Springfield, VA 22150
800-217-3526
ladyriderswear@juno.com
www.ladyriderswear.com

Mota
1477 San Pablo Ave.
Berkeley, CA 94702
510-527-6804
888-539-MOTA
info@motagear.com
www.motagear.com

WomanBiker.com
PMB 274, 26 S. Main St.
Concord, NH 03301
603-226-5859
877-WM-BIKER
www.womanbiker.com

Apparel—General (includes women's lines and sizes)

Aerostich Riderwearhouse
8 S. 18th Ave. W.
Duluth, MN 55806
218-722-1927
800-222-1994
www.aerostich.com

Brooks Leather Sportswear
13311 North End
Oak Park, MI 48237
800-727-6657

Fieldsheer
485 E. 17 St. Ste. 400
Costa Mesa, CA 92627
949-642-6877

Gypsy Leather
71 Saint John St.
Lancaster, NY 14086
800-63-GYPSY
www.gypsyleather.com

Harley-Davidson
  MotorClothes
3700 W. Juneau Ave.
P.O. Box 653
Milwaukee, WI 53201
800-443-2153

Intersport Fashions
333 S. Anita Dr. Ste. 1025
Orange, CA 92668
www.intersportfashions.com

Iron Horse Clothing
21607 SE Frontage Rd.
Joliet, IL 60436
800-784-8401
www.ironhorseclothing.com

Kneedraggers.com
www.kneedraggers.com
Racing gear.

Langlitz Leathers
2440 SE Division
Portland, OR 97202
503-235-0959
www.langlitz.com

Motoport USA
750 N. Citracado Pkwy.
  Ste. 17
Escondido, CA 92029
800-777-6499
www.motoport.com

Orchard Leathers
36-06 43rd Ave.
Long Island City, NY 11101
718-361-2072
800-BRANDED
www.800branded.com

Schott Brothers
358 Lehigh Ave.
Perth Amboy, NJ 08862
800-25-SCHOTT

S&S Cycle & Supply
304 Rolling Trail
Amarillo, TX 79108
806-355-8541
800-321-2735

Thurlow Leatherworld
4807 Mercury St. Ste. E
San Diego, CA 92111
800-627-7954

TourMaster (Helmet House)
2360 Townsgate Rd.
Westlake Village, CA 91361
805-373-6868
800-421-7247
www.tourmaster.com

Vanguard Leather
258 Broadhollow Rd.
P.O. Box 3208
Farmingdale, NY 11735
516-420-1010

Vanson USA
951 Broadway
Fall River, MA 02724
508-678-2000
www.vansonleathers.com

Vent-Tech Leathers
1106 Oceannaire Dr. Ste. J
Glendale, CA 91208
800-331-8408

Apparel—Boots

Dayton Shoe Co.
2250 E. Hastings St.
Vancouver, BC V5L 1V4
CANADA
604-253-6671
800-342-8934
www.daytonshoe.com

West Coast Shoe Co.
P.O. Box 607
Scappoose, OR 97056-0607
503-543-7114
800-326-2711
www.westcoastshoe.com

Custom fitting.

Heated Apparel

Gerbings Heated Clothing
E750 Dalby Rd.
Union, WA 98592
360-898-4225
800-646-5916
www.gerbing.com

Eclipse
3771 E. Ellsworth Rd.
Ann Arbor, MI 48108
800-666-1500
www.eclipseluggage.com

Widder Enterprises
942 E. Ojai Ave.
Ojai, CA 93023
805-640-1295
800-WYBCOLD
www.widder.com

Rain Gear

Dry Rider
Neese Industries
P.O. Box 1059
Gonzales, LA 70707
800-535-8042
www.neeseind.com

Thunderwear
951-B Calle Negocio
San Clemente, CA 92672
714-492-1141
800-422-6565

TourMaster
800-445-2552
www.tourmaster.com

ASSOCIATIONS AND FOUNDATIONS

Associations—Women's

Women's Int'l Motorcycle
   Association (WIMA)
6 Stottingway St.
Upwey, Weymouth
Dorset DT3 5QA
44-1305-812051
Sheonagh Ravensdale, Pres.
Sheonagh_ravensdale
   @compuserve.com
wimagb@wima-gb.co.uk
www.wima-gb.co.uk

Founded by American Louise Scherbyn in 1950 primarily as a correspondence club, WIMA now hosts international rallies. There are 2,000 members in 14 countries worldwide. U.S. clubs are invited to join the WIMA network.

Associations—Women's (Cont'd)

Women's Motorcyclist
  Foundation (WMF)
Sue Slate and Gin Shear, Dirs.
7 Lent Ave.
LeRoy, NY 14482
716-768-6054
800-442-3550, ext. 6116
wmfginsue@aol.com
www.ponyexpress2000.org

A non-profit networking
group with 300–500 mem-
bers. "Diversity is welcomed
as a way to enrich our lives."
Est. 1983 to inspire women to
ride, and to improve riding
and mechanical skills. WMF
organizes Pony Express and
other Road to a Cure benefits
for breast cancer research.
Publication: *Journey of Hope.*

Women Motorcyclists of
  Southern California (WMSC)
P.O. Box 292135
Los Angeles, CA 90029-8635
213-483-4665
womenmoto@earthlink.net
http://home.earthlink.net/
  ~womenmoto/index.html

"An umbrella organization for
women riders of all ages, colors and occupations. Our
goals are to change the negative views that have been cast
upon motorcyclists." WMSC
runs group rides for all levels
and organizes women to participate in other events, including charity benefits.

Associations—General

American Bikers Aimed
  Toward Education (ABATE)
ABATE works for bikers'
rights. To find your nearest
state office, inquire at your
AMA district office, local bike
shops, or regional publications.

American Motorcyclist
  Association (AMA)
13515 Yarmouth Dr.
Pickerington, OH 43147
614-856-1900
800-AMA-JOIN
www.ama-cycle.org

A not-for-profit organization
that convenes riding tours,
sanctions competitive events,
lobbies for bikers' rights, pub-
lishes a magazine, runs a museum, and offers other perks
to its 260,000 members (as of
2000, 7% are women).

Canadian Motorcycle
  Association
Box 448
Hamilton, ON L8L 8C4
CANADA
905-522-5705
www.canmocycle.ca

Discover Today's
  Motorcycling (DTM)
2 Jenner St. Ste. 150
Irvine, CA 92718
949-727-4211
800-833-3995
www.mic.org

Associations—General (Cont'd)

Motorcycle Industry Council
2 Jenner St. Ste. 150
Irvine, CA 92718
949-727-4211
www.mic.org

Trade organization.

Motorcycle Riders
  Foundation (MRF)
Wayne Curtin, Nat'l Director
P.O. Box 1808
Washington, DC 20013-1808
202-546-0983

National Coalition of
  Motorcyclists (NCOM)
15910 Ventura Blvd.
Encino, CA 91436
800-525-5355 (USA)
800-521-2425 (CAN)

BOOKS AND VIDEOS

Books and Videos—Distributors

Classic Motorbooks
P.O. Box 1
Osceola, WI 54020
800-826-6600
www.motorbooks.com

Transportation book
specialists.

Garage Company
13211 Washington Blvd.
Los Angeles, CA 90066
310-821-1793
www.garagecompany.com

Vintage (rare) books and
memorabilia.

Hosking Bookworks
136 Hosking Ln.
Accord, NY 12404
800-626-4231
www.hoskingcycle.com

Back issue magazines.

Whitehorse Press
P.O. Box 60
N. Conway, NH 03860-0060
800-531-1133
www.whitehorsepress.com

The largest selection of books
and videos for motorcyclists.

Books—Recommended Titles

*Cooking with the
  Two Fat Ladies*
by Jennifer Paterson and
  Clarissa Dickson Wright.
(Random House, 1998)

The "doyennes of decadent
food" rode the British coun-
tryside on their Triumph 950
with sidecar to gather time-
tested recipes. *Two Fat Ladies
Full Throttle* was published by
Clarkson Potter in 1999.

*Flaming Iguanas: An
  Illustrated All-Girl Road
  Novel Thing*
by Erika Lopez
(Simon & Schuster, 1997)

Spicy, funny fiction with car-
toons about the adventures of
Tomato Rodriquez, a bisexual, Puerto Rican biker chick.

Iron-Horse Cowgirls
  (working title)
by Linda Back McKay.

Stories of women riders exploring other areas of their
lives besides motorcycling.
Collected via e-mail, this
compilation includes women
from outside North America.
Publication circa 2001–2.

Books—Recommended Titles (Cont'd)

Motorcycling Excellence: Skills, Knowledge and Strategies for Riding Right
by the Motorcycle Safety Foundation
(Whitehorse Press, 1995)

"The more you know, the better it gets."

Motorcycles: Fundamentals, Service, Repair
by Bruce Johns and David Edmundson
(Goodheart-Willcox, 1987)

Motorcycle Touring and Travel: A Handbook of Travel by Motorcycle, 2nd Ed.
by Bill Stermer
(Whitehorse Press, 1999)

A nuts and bolts guide to planning and packing for the road.

On the Perimeter
by Hazel Kolb with Bill Stermer
(Maverick, 1983)

Kolb's autobiography chronicling her ride around the U.S. perimeter. Well-written and riveting. Out-of-print but worth finding.

The Perfect Vehicle: What It Is About Motorcycles
by Melissa Holbrook Pierson
(W.W. Norton, 1997)

Nicely written, occasionally melancholy essays about the author's perceptions of motorcycling and her experiences on her Moto Guzzi. Parts are reprinted magazine articles.

A Twist of the Wrist
by Keith Code.

Two books and a video from the California Superbike School; see RIDER TRAINING.

Videos—Recommended Titles

Motorcycle Diaries
Diva Films
c/o Cinema Guild
1697 Broadway #506
New York, NY 10019
212-246-5522
dhowells@mssnyc.com
www.divafilms.com

Two women ride the U.S. East Coast to interview female racers and riders.

Secret History of Bikers
TLC Video
Los Angeles, CA
www.tlc.com

Entertaining, accurate history of American motorcycling with a significant segment on women.

She Lives to Ride
Filkela Films
539 Tremont St. Ste. 409
Boston, MA 02116
617-542-7699

Fine documentary about five diverse women riders.

Street Smarts I, II, & III
Whitehorse Press
P.O. Box 60
N. Conway, NH 03860-0060
800-531-1133
www.whitehorsepress.com

Urban street riding strategies.

Women & Motorcycling National Conference

Workshops, seminars and other events of the AMA conferences on several videos. See AMA in ASSOCIATIONS.

CLUBS

Clubs—Women's International and National

The beauty of women's motorcycle clubs is that most welcome diversity. Individual chapters of the national organizations, and independent clubs listed in subsequent sections, range from upscale professionals who have time to ride together only once a month, to lifestyle bikers who live and breathe bikes. Many groups organize events for charities. Most clubs welcome all women, including passenger riders and those who would like to learn more about the sport.

Ladies of Harley (LOH)
3700 W. Juneau Ave.
Milwaukee, WI 53201
414-343-4515 (USA)
414-343-4896 (Int'l.)
800-CLUB-HOG
www.hog.com

LOH is part of Harley Owners Group (HOG) and membership is automatic with purchase of a new Harley. Of HOG's 500,000 members worldwide, about 72,000 are LOH (riders and passengers). Est. 1986. HOG Rallies are held throughout the world. Publications: *HOG Tales, Enthusiast, Ladies of Harley Cookbook.* (The latter is available through LOH of Anchorage, AK, www.alaskan.com/ladiesofharley. Proceeds to charity.)

Motor Maids
P.O. Box 1664
Englewood, FL 34295
941-474-3970
Jan Barrett, President
motormaidsinc@juno.com
www.motormaids.org

About 500 members mainly in the U.S. Some members in Canada and Australia. All types of bikes. "We are women who RIDE. We are committed to promoting a positive image of motorcycling to our community." Est. 1940. Chapters in different parts of the country host an annual convention, during which members parade in uniform. Motor Maids must be AMA members. Publications: Advisory newsletter; *Celebration Journal* (tribute to the late Dot Robinson, former Motor Maids president and sidecar racer; contains memoirs from those who knew and loved her).

Women in the Wind (WITW)
P.O. Box 8392
Toledo, OH 43605
Becky Brown, Founder
witwusa@aol.com
Gale Collins, President
nchogmom@aol.com
http://free.prohosting.com/~witw/

More than 800 members in 50 chapters, mainly in the U.S.; also chapters in Canada, England, Sweden, Australia, and New Zealand. "Has motorcycling fever grabbed you tightly leaving no space for anything else in your life? Looking for other women to share your love of the road and the wind? Look no further." Lots of Harleys but all bikes welcome. Chapter independence and individualism are encouraged, while still belonging to the larger family. Est. 1979. Summer and Winter Nationals are hosted each year by chapters in different parts of the country. Newsletter: *Shootin' the Breeze.*

Clubs—Women's International and National (Cont'd)

Women on Wheels (WOW)
P.O. Box 26
Fall River, WI 53932-0026
800-322-1969
general@womenonwheels.org
membership
  @womenonwheels.org
www.womenonwheels.org

More than 2,000 members riding all types of bikes; 60 chapters in 30 U.S. states; one chapter in New Brunswick, Canada; individual members in several other countries. "If you are a lady who loves to drive or ride pillion (as passenger) on motorcycles, motorbikes, scooters, or trikes, this is the group for you! Our mission: To unite all women motorcycle enthusiasts for recreation, education, mutual support, recognition, and to promote a positive image of motorcycling." Est. 1982. International Ride-In takes place in a different part of the country each year; there are several regional rallies and WOW-WOWs (women-only weekends). Magazine: *Women on Wheels.*

Clubs—Women's Independent Regional, Local

Regional and local clubs are forming continuously. Consult periodicals such as *Woman Rider*, women's e-zines listed in this directory, and web sites of sources such as the American Motorcyclist Association and MotorcycleWorld.com for new groups. Local dealerships are sources for club news. Here's a sampling:

Desert Hearts
Phoenix, AZ
602-279-9228
Deb Lotardo, Founder
deserteheartsmc@home.com
www.desertheartsmc.com

"We are women who want to ride together in a comfortable, fun, and safe environment. We have NO political or other agenda."

Kat's Bike Club for Women
Scranton/Wilkes Barre, PA
Kittykat47@hotmail.com

"A group where women and girls can have fun while sharing experiences and their love of motorcycles."

Lady Riders
Mary Ann Kent
120 Pepperidge Place
Sterling, VA 20164

Leather & Lace
800-526-LACE
laceone@aol.com
lacepa@aol.com
www.leatherandlacemc.com

Bay State and PA chapters. Emphasis on Harley lifestyle. "Leather stands for our inner strength, lace depicts our femininity. When you get tired of riding in the back and making the potato salad, give us a call."

North American Amazons
www.amazonsmc.com
amazons@amazonsmc.com

Individual members across the U.S. and Canada. "We are a fun-loving breed, a sisterhood who love to ride and want to share that rush."

Pennsylvania Motorcyclist
  Society (PMS)
pmsbiker@geocities.com
www.geocities.com/wellesley/
  1305/index.html

"If you are a woman with an open mind, join us for rides and friendship. We welcome diversity. Our goal is to find the best ice cream within a day's ride of SW Penn."

Clubs—Women's Independent Regional, Local (Cont'd)

Raw Silk
San Francisco Bay area
webmistress@rawsilkmc.com
www.angelfire.com/ca/
   rawsilkmc/

"Joy in riding, pride in living clean & sober."

Sisters Motorcycle Club
Montpelier, VT
kimb@motorcycleworld.com

"Sistercentral for VT women motorcyclists."

Spokes-Women
57 Orchid Lane
Brick, NJ 08724
Liz Smith, President
732-714-7650
esmith3@telecordia.com
www.spokes-women.org

"We want to change the way you think about motorcycling."

Twin Rose Lady Riders
214 Ruby St.
Lancaster, PA 17603

Women of Diamonds & Chrome
P.O. Box 99
Saginaw, MO 64864
Roberta Jeffries
417-623-5432
nature@clandjop.com

Clubs—Women of Color

Ebony Queens
P.O. Box 311021
Flint, MI 48504
"Pie," President
616-452-7306
pieeqmc1@prodigy.net

"All shades of fine (all women welcome). We promote safe and adventurous motorcycling."

Lady Hawks
15475 Homeland Dr.
Hughesville, MD 20637
Paula Dove, President
301-870-0572
fdove@sprynet.com

"We are a group of multi-cultural, multi-racial female riders united to promote motorcycle awareness and camaraderie."

Clubs—Lesbian

Artemis
c/o Alex Davis
P.O. Box 431
Parker Ford, PA 19457
610-495-2221
amagic1100@aol.com
artemismc@aol.com

Chapters in Philadelphia area and Haddon Township, NJ.

Moving Violations
c/o Kristine Grimes
18 Chandler St., #2
Somerville, MA 02144
617-627-9257
dedhedbykr@aol.com

New Mexico Sirens
c/o Maria Bautista
P.O. Box 28104
Santa Fe, NM 87592
505-424-9189
lunar@rt66.com

Not affiliated with the NY and SF Sirens.

Clubs—Lesbian (Cont'd)

Sirens
One Little West 12th St.
New York, NY 10014
212-749-6177
718-857-8704 (general info)
Jacqui Sturgess
sirennyc@aol.com
www.sirensnyc.com

Predominantly lesbian; all women welcome. Mission: "To promote motorcycling as a sport among women emphasizing safety, solidarity, support and friendship." Chapters in New York and San Francisco.

Clubs—Male and Female Members

There are thousands of regional, local, brand-specific, and specialty clubs, and new groups are forming continuously. Consult periodicals such as *Rider, Motorcycle Consumer News,* and web sites of sources like the American Motorcyclist Association and MotorcycleWorld.com for new groups. Local dealerships are sources for club news, and motorcycle manufacturers can point you to owners' groups. Here's a sampling to whet your appetite:

Antique Motorcycle Club of
America
P.O. Box 330H
Sweetster, IN 46987
800-782-2622
www.antiquemotorcycle.org

Association of Recovering
Motorcyclists (ARM)
1503 Market St.
La Crosse, WI 54601
608-784-8462
www.armintl86@aol.com

BMW Motorcycle Owners of
America (BMWMOA)
P.O. Box 489
Chesterfield, MO 63006-
0489
636-537-5511
www.bmwmoa.org

BMW Riders Association
(BMWRA)
P.O. Box 510309
Melbourne, FL 32951-0309
407-984-7800
www.bmwra.org

Blue Knights International
Law Enforcement M/C
38 Alden St.
Bangor, ME 04401
207-947-4600
www.blueknights.org

Buell Riders Adventure
Group (BRAG)
3700 W. Juneau Ave.
Milwaukee, WI 53208
888-432-BRAG
brag@buell.com

Christian Motorcyclist
Association (CMA)
P.O. Box 9
Hatfield, AZ 71945
501-389-6196
cmaus@aol.com
www.cma-wa.com

Concours Owners Group
P.O. Box 0505
Acme, MI 49610
www.concours.org

Gold Wing Road Riders
Association (GWRRA)
21423 N. 11th Ave.
Phoenix, AZ 85027
602-581-2500
800-843-9460
www.gwrra.org

Clubs—Male and Female Members (Cont'd)

Harley Owners Group
 (HOG)
See Ladies of Harley.

Honda Riders Club of
 America (HRCA)
American Honda Motor Co.
P.O. Box 3976
Gardena, CA 90247
800-847-HRCA

Indian Motorcycle Club of
 America
P.O. Box 1743
Perris, CA 92370-1743

International Brotherhood of
 Motorcycle Campers
P.O. Box 2395
Chandler, AZ 85244-2395
480-963-6992

Italian Motorcycle
 Owners Club
P.O. Box 332
Brooklyn, CT 06234
203-774-8365

Knights of Life
P.O. Box 144
Livingston, NJ 07039
908-322-7200
www.cmhfins@sprynet.com

Health care professionals.

Moto Guzzi National
 Owners Club
P.O. Box 98
Olmitz, KS 67564
316-586-3275

Retreads Motorcycle Club
 International
http://home.hiwaay.net/
pvteye/retreads.html

For riders over age 40; 24,000
members in 50 states, Canada,
Europe.

Spanish Motorcycle Owners
 Group (SMOG)
1320 Cathy Lane
Minden, NV 89423
702-267-2103

Sportys
Assn. of Sportster Enthusiasts
P.O. Box 593
E. Bridgewater, MA 02333-
 0593
508-378-2233

Triumph International
 Owners Club
P.O. Box 6676
Holliston, MA 01746-6676
508-429-4221

United Sidecar Association
130 S. Michigan Ave.
Villa Park, IL 50181

Virago Owners Club
6785 S. Threshold Pt.
Homosassa, FL 34446
800-315-3209
www.xtalwind.net/~virago/

Yamaha 650 Society
P.O. Box 234
O'Fallon, MO 63366-0234

EMERGENCY SERVICES AND ROADSIDE ASSISTANCE

In addition to the services listed below, many clubs offer similar programs. Check out the following organizations in CLUBS: BMW Motorcycle Owners of America, BMW Riders Association, Gold Wing Road Riders Association, Harley Owner's Group, and the Honda Riders Club of America.

Accident Scene
 Management
P.O. Box 552
Wausau, WI 54402
vroberts@pcpros.net
www.accidentscene.net

"Crash Course for the Motorcyclist," taught by an RN/
EMT; what to do until help
arrives. "Trauma Packs" with
survival items also available.

Emergency Services and Roadside Assistance (Cont'd)

International Help'n' Hands
See AMA in ASSOCIATIONS.

Motorcycle Towing Service
  (MTS)
4180 S. Pecos Ste. 105
Las Vegas, NV 89121
800-999-7064
www.mtstowing.com

Shell Motorist Club
929 N. Plum Grove Rd.
Schaumburg, IL 60173
800-852-0555

HELMETS

Also see ACCESSORIES—General. Note: *Motorcyclist* magazine does an annual comparison of full-face helmets for comfort, weight, how much wind noise they let in, etc.

AGV, Inc.
7311 Grove Rd.
Frederick, MD 21701
800-950-9006
www.agv.com.english/us

Arai
P.O. Box 9485
Daytona, FL 32120
800-766-ARAI (dealer locator)
www.araiamericas.com

Bell
5331 Santa Catalina Ave.
Garden Grove, CA 92645
800-848-3879
www.bellhelmets.com

Arthur Fulmer
122 Gayoso Ave.
Memphis, TN 38103
901-525-5711

Lazer
P.O. Box 279
1125 Pecan Dr.
Bellvue, CO 80512
303-482-6623
800-321-6621
www.lazerhelmets.com

Nolan
CIMA International
284 N. Main
Glen Ellyn, IL 60137
630-690-3162

Shoei
371 Elizabeth Ln. Ste. 100
Corona, CA 92880
909-520-0500
www.shoei-helments.com

Team Simpson Race Products
329 FM 306
New Braunfels, TX 78130
800-621-6507
www.simpsonraceproducts.
  com

MECHANICS' SCHOOLS

American Motorcycle
  Institute (AMI)
3042 International
  Speedway Blvd.
Daytona Beach, FL 32124
904-255-0295
800-881-2-AMI
www.amiwrench.com

Motorcycle Mechanics
  Institute (MMI)
2844 W. Deer Valley Rd.
Phoenix, AZ 85027
602-869-9644 (AZ)
407-240-2422 (FL)
800-528-7995

MOTORCYCLE MANUFACTURERS

American Dirt Bike
5430 Union Pacific Ave.
City of Commerce, CA
 90022
213-722-8880
800-426-6869

Aprilla, Montesa, Scorpa
800-877-APRILLA

ATK USA
1164 W. 850 N.
Centerville, UT 84014
801-298-8288
800-285-8724
www.atkusa.com

BMW of North America
300 Chestnut Ridge Rd.
Woodcliff Lake, NJ 07675
800-345-4-BMW (dealer info)
www.bmwusa.com

Buell Motor Co.
214 Jefferson St.
Wukwonago, WI 53149
800-490-9635 (dealer info)
www.buell.com

Ducati
888-DUCATI-2
www.ducatiusa.com

Cobra Motorcycle Mfg.
714-779-7798
www.cobrausa.com

Harley-Davidson
 Motor Co.
3700 W. Juneau Ave.
P.O. Box 653
Milwaukee, WI 53201
414-342-4680
800-443-2153 (dealer info)

American Honda Motor Co.
1919 Torrance Blvd.
Torrance, CA 90501-2746
310-783-2000

Indian
800-445-1759
www.indianmotorcycle.com

American Jawa Ltd.
185 Express St.
Plainview, NY 11803
516-938-3210
www.zeton.com

Kawasaki Motors Corp., USA
9950 Jeronimo Rd.
Irvine, CA 92718
714-770-0400
800-661-RIDE
www.kawasaki.com

Moto America
(Moto Guzzi)
445 W. Depot St.
Angier, NC 27501
800-USA-MOTO
www.motoguzzi-us.com

Moto Morini
Herdan Corp.
Rte. 61 Box 65
Port Clinton, PA 19549
610-562-3155
www.herdan.com

Rokon International
140 West Rd.
Portsmouth, NH 03801
603-431-5100
www.rokon.com

Royal Enfield Classic
 Motorworks
800-201-7472
www.enfieldmotorcycles.com

American Suzuki
 Motor Corp.
3251 E. Imperial Hwy.
Brea, CA 92621
714-996-7040
800-828-RIDE
www.suzuki.com

Triumph USA
403 Dividend Dr.
Peachtree City, GA 30269
770-631-9500
800-RIDE-TRI
www.triumph.co.uk

Ural America
P.O. Box 969
Preston, WA 98050
800-832-2845
www.ural.com

Motorcycle Manufacturers (Cont'd)

Victory Polaris
800-785-2747
www.victory-usa.com

Yamaha Motor Corp. USA
6555 Katella Ave.
Cypress, CA 90630
714-761-7300
800-88-YAMAHA (dealer info)
www.yamaha-motor.com

MUSEUMS

Barbour Vintage Motorsports
  Museum
2721 5th Ave. S.
Birmingham, AL 35210

Harley-Davidson Museum
1425 Eden Rd.
York, PA 17402
717-848-1177

Indian Motocycle Museum
33 Hendee St.
Springfield, MA 01109
413-737-2624

Motorcycle Hall of Fame
See AMA in ASSOCIATIONS.

National Motorcycle
  Museum and Hall of Fame
P.O. Box 602
1650 Lavelle
Sturgis, SD 57785
605-347-4875
www.museum.sturgis-
  rally.com

Petersen Automotive
  Museum
6060 Wilshire Blvd.
Los Angeles, CA 90036
323-930-2277

Trev Deeley Motorcycle
  Museum
13500 Verdun Pl.
Richmond, BC V6V 1V2
CANADA
604-273-5421

Wheels Through Time
  Museum
1121B Veteran's
  Memorial Dr.
Mt. Vernon, IL 62864
618-244-4118

PERIODICALS

Periodicals—Women's On-line (e-zines)

Women of the Road
www.womenoftheroad.com
Alyn Shannon, Editor
alyn@dqi.net

Letters, forum, events, poetry, personals. The editor's 1995 Harley lifestyle photo essay, *Women of the Road,* is sold through the site. Light on text but the photos say it all.

Periodicals—Women's Print

Note: The major women's clubs publish informative and fun magazines or newsletters in print or on-line. Many smaller clubs have newsletters and web sites, too.

Biker Alley
299 Hill Ave.
Bartlett, IL 60103
630-837-6490
Renate ("Rain")
  Nietzold, Editor
bniet@aol.com

Bikes & Spikes
P.O. Box 15669
Minneapolis, MN 55415
800-862-2307, access 00
denise@bikesandspikes.com
www.bikesandspikes.com

Slightly raunchy but fun Harley lifestyle stuff: tattoos, beefcake pix, personals.

MotoMama
452 W. 19 St., Ste. 1D
New York, NY 10011
Jennifer Palmer, Publisher
646-486-1878
info@motomama.com
www.motomama.com

"Magazine for Biker Chicks" is the subtitle of this saucy magazine for street and sport riders. Profiles, product reviews, editorials, etc.

Woman Rider
6420 Sycamore Ln.
Maple Grove, MN 55369
888-269-0963 (editorial)
877-427-1356 (subscriptions)
Genevieve Schmitt, Editor
womanrider1@aol.com

Launched in 2000, *Woman Rider* is a well-rounded magazine for women riding all brands. It grew out of the now-defunct *Asphalt Angels,* which began life as *Harley Women.* Road tests, product reviews, events, profiles, etc.

Periodicals—General On-Line

Cybercycle
www.motorcycleworld.com
Kim Brittenham, Editor
kbrittenham
  @motorcycleworld.com

News, profiles, product and book reviews, plus a women's section with a forum and events.

E-SportBike
www.esportbike.com

Interactive Motorcycle
www.activebike.com

"Lexicon of the thinking rider." Features, fiction, opinions.

Motorcycle Madness
www.motorcyclemadness.org

Features, message boards, events.

Motorcycle On-Line Magazine
www.motorcycle.com/
  motorcycle.html

"The world's first all-digital motorcycle magazine" News, products, tech, racing.

2WF.com
www.2wf.com

Periodicals—General Print

The major motorcycle magazines are excellent sources for road tests, tech and safety tips, news of rallies and other events, and reviews and ads for just about every product for bike and rider. National magazines with female editors are indicated. Check dealerships and biker gathering spots for local papers, which are often free and great sources for rides and events.

American Iron
1010 Summer St.
Stamford, CT 06905
203-855-0008
800-875-2997
www.americaniron.com

American Motorcyclist
Comes with AMA membership; see AMA in ASSOCIATIONS.

American Rider
TL Enterprises
2575 Vista Del Mar Dr.
Ventura, CA 93001
805-667-4196

American Roadracing
1310 W. Colonial Dr.
Orlando, FL 32804
407-481-2979
www.americanroadracing.com

BlackRiders Magazine
P.O. Box 58
4320 Hamilton St.
Hyattsville, MD 20781

BMW ON (Owners News)
Sandy Cohen, Editor
Available with BMWMOA membership; see CLUBS.

Cruising Rider
6420 Sycamore Lane Ste. 100
Maple Grove, MN 55369
www.ehlertpowersports.com

Cycle News
2201 Cherry Ave.
Long Beach, CA 90806
800-831-2220
www.cyclenews.com

Cycle World
1499 Monrovia Ave.
Newport Beach, CA 92663
949-720-5300

Dirt Rider
6420 Wilshire Blvd.
Los Angeles, CA 90048-5515
323-782-2000

Easyriders
Paisano Publications
P.O. Box 469054
Escondido, CA 92046
888-805-5999

Adult content.

Enthusiast
Harley-Davidson Motor Co.
3700 W. Juneau Ave.
P.O. Box 653
Milwaukee, WI 53201
414-342-4680

Hack'd
P.O. Box 813
Buckhannon, WV 26201
304-472-6146

Sidecars.

Iron Works
P.O. Box 1096
Morganton, NC 28680-1096
334-834-1170
www.ironworksmag.com

Motorcycle Consumer News
P.O. Box 6050
Mission Viejo, CA 92690
949-855-8822
www.mcnews.com

Motorcycle Cruiser
See *Dirt Rider.*
mcccsubs@emapusa.com

Motorcycle Events
P.O. Box 100
Pierre, SD 57501
605-945-2986
888-700-8855
Sally Reiman, Editor
sally@motorcycleevents.com
www.motorcycleevents.com

Periodicals—General Print (Cont'd)

Motorcycle Industry
 Magazine
P.O. Box 160
1267 Hwy 395 N.
Gardnerville, NV 89410
752-782-0222

Motorcycle Shopper
1353 Herndon Ave.
Deltona, FL 32725-9046
407-860-1989

Motorcycle Tour & Cruiser
1010 Summer St.
Stamford, CT 06905
203-855-0008
800-875-2997
Laura Brengelman, Editor
mtcmagazine@earthlink.net

Motorsport
550 Honey Locust Rd.
Jonesburg, MO 63351-9600
314-488-3113

Motorcyclist
323-782-2230
See Dirt Rider.

MX Action/Dirt Bike
P.O. Box 958
Valencia, CA 91380
800-767-0345
www.dirtbikemagazine.com
www.motocrossactionmag.
com

NADA Appraisal Guides
P.O. Box 7800
Costa Mesa, CA 92628
888-232-6232
www.nadaguides.com

Used motorcycles.

Old Bike Journal
See American Iron.

Rider
2575 Vista del Mar Dr.
Ventura, CA 93001
805-667-4196

Roadracing World &
 Motorcycle Technology
581-C Birch St.
Lake Elsinore, CA 92530
909-245-6411
www.roadracingworld.com

The Sidecarist
See United Sidecar Association in CLUBS.

Sport Rider
213-782-2584
See Dirt Rider.

Street Bike
1339 Mission St.
San Francisco, CA 94103
415-252-6669
www.streetbikemagazine.com

Walneck's Classic Cycle Trader
P.O. Box 420
Mt. Morris, IL 61054
800-877-6141
www.traderonline.com

RACE SANCTIONING ORGANIZATIONS

The AMA sanctions many forms of amateur and pro competition, including drag racing, motocross, road racing, enduro (cross-country), hillclimbing, and more. See AMA in ASSOCIATIONS.

All-Harley Drag Racing Assn.
Dane Miller, President
P.O. Box 11845
Winston-Salem, NC 27116
336-924-2095
www.ahdra.com

AMA-ProStar
Keith Kizer
P.O. Box 18039
Huntsville, AL 35804
256-852-1101
www.amaprostar.com

All brands.

American Federation of
 Motorcyclists (AFM)
P.O. Box 5018-333
Newark, CA 94560
510-796-7005

Road racing.

Race Sanctioning Organizations (Cont'd)

American Historic Racing
  Motorcycle Association
  (AHRMA)
P.O. Box L
Mt. Jewett, PA 16740-0554
814-778-2291
www.ahrma.org

American Motorcycle
  Racing Association (AMRA)
Richard Wegner, President
Box 50
Itasca, IL 60143
630-250-0838
All-Harley drags.

International Drag Bike
  Association
3936 Raceway Park Rd.
Mt. Olive, AL 35117
205-849-7886
www.idba.com

National Hot Rod Assn.
P.O. Box 5555
Glendora, CA 91740
626-963-7695
626-914-4836
www.nhra.com
Pro stock bikes.

Western Eastern Racing
  Association (WERA)
2555 Marietta Hwy. #104
Canton, GA 30114
770-720-5010
www.wera.com
Road Racing.

RALLIES, RIDES, EVENTS

There are scores of rallies. At the start of each riding season, magazines such as *Rider, Motorcycle Tour & Cruiser,* and *Motorcycle Events* publish calendars of rallies and events. The AMA also hosts various events throughout the season. See AMA in ASSOCIATIONS.

Rallies, Rides, Events—Women's

Catskills Women's
  Motorcycle Festival
Contact: Rayla Hart
P.O. Box 146
West Shokan, NY 12494
914-657-6227
womenride@aol.com

Mid-Atlantic Women's
  Motorcycle Rally (June)
P.O. Box 290
Bel Air, MD 21014-0290
410-850-8528
www.mawmr.com
For breast cancer research.

Women's Motorcyclist
  Foundation (various events)
wmfginsue@aol.com
800-442-3550, ex. 6116
Breast cancer benefit events,
and gatherings for riding and
mechanical skills.

Ladies of Harley
1-800-CLUB-HOG
www.hog.com
Various events at HOG
gatherings.

Motor Maids
  Convention (Summer)
941-474-3970
motormaidsinc@juno.com
www.motormaids.org

Women's International
  Motorcycle Association
44-1305-812051
Sheonagh_ravensdale
  @compuserve.com
www.wima-gb.co.uk
Various events in different
countries.

Rallies, Rides, Events—Women's (Cont'd)

Women in the Wind
  Nationals (July, Feb)
witwusa@aol.com
http://free.prohosting.com/
  ~witw/

Women on Wheels
  International Ride-In (July)
800-322-1969
general
  @womenonwheels.org
www.womenonwheels.org

Rallies, Rides, and Events—General

Americade (June)
P.O. Box 2205
Glens Falls, NY 12801
518-798-7888
www.tourexpo.com

Bike Week (March)
Daytona Beach, FL
800-854-1234
www.daytonabeach.com

Biketoberfest (Oct.)
Daytona Beach, FL
800-854-1234
www.biketoberfest.org

BMW Motorcycle Owners of
  America Int'l Rally (July)
See BMWMOA in CLUBS.

BMW Riders Association
  Int'l Rally (Aug.)
See BMWRA in CLUBS.

Harley Owners Group Rallies
See HOG in CLUBS.

Honda Hoot (June)
www.hondahoot.com
See HRCA in CLUBS

Int'l Motorcycle Shows
Avanstar Expositions
800-331-5706

Off-season consumer expos in
various cities.

Laconia Rally & Race
  Week (June)
Laconia, NH
603-366-2000
www.laconiamcweek.com

Love Ride (Nov.)
Harley-Davidson of
  Glendale
3717 San Fernando Rd.
Glendale, CA 91204
818-246-5618
www.loveride.org

Benefits the Muscular
Dystrophy Association.

Nat'l Bikers Roundup (Aug.)
Contact Nona ("Li'l Taco")
  Alexander
713-733-5927

Primarily African-American
riders; hosted by a different
club each year.

Rolling Thunder
  Ride for Freedom
  (Memorial Day Weekend)
Artie Muller, Nat'l Chapter
P.O. Box 216
Neshantic Sta., NJ 08853-
  0216

Ride to the Vietnam Veteran's
Memorial in Washington,
D.C.

Sturgis Rally & Races (Aug.)
  a/k/a Black Hills
  Motor Classic
P.O. Box 189
Sturgis, SD 57785
605-347-6570
www.rally.sturgis.sd.us

Vintage Motorcycle Days
(July)
See AMA in ASSOCIATIONS.

RIDER TRAINING

California's Leading
  Advanced Safety School
  (CLASS)
15500 W. Telegraph Rd.
  Ste. C24
Santa Paula, CA 93060
805-933-9936
www.classrides.com

Taught at the racetrack but applicable to the street. Some women-only track days.

Debbie Matthews' Women's
  School of Motocross
949-837-2206
deb@dmsports-wsmx.com
www.dmsports-wsmx.com

"A school strong enough for men . . . but made for women!" All levels. Schools in CA, NV, WA, CO, TX, WV. Plus free schools given anywhere in the U.S. for groups of 10 or more.

DP Safety School
Morro Bay, CA
805-772-8301
www.dpsafetyschool.com

Ducati Track Day
  for Women
New Hampshire
  International Speedway
Louden, NH
Susie@bcmducati.com
www.bcmducati.com

Ed Bargy Racing Services
P.O. Box 250222
Atlanta, GA 30325
404-352-5750

Frank Hawley's NHRA
  Drag Racing School
P.O. Box 484
La Verne, CA 91750-0484
909-622-2466
888-901-7223
www.racingschools.com/
  ~schools/hawley/index.html

Hardly Angels Women's
  Motorcycle Drill Team
Cheryl Bellino
838 County Rd. 233
Durango, CO 81301
970-247-5276
bellino@frontier.net
lynell@frontier.net
www.hardlyangels.com

"The Chorus Line on Wheels." A performing group which promotes skills through entertainment.

Harley-Davidson
  Academy of Motorcycling
  Rider's Edge Course
www.ridersedge.com

The MSF Beginner Course taught on 500cc Buell Blasts.

Keith Code's California
  Superbike School
P.O. Box 3601
Glendale, CA 91201
800-530-3350
818-841-7661
www.superbikeschool.com
Some women-only track days.

Lawrence Grodsky's Stayin'
  Safe Motorcycle Training
P.O. Box 81810
Pittsburgh, PA 15217
412-421-5711
www.stayinsafe.com

Motorcycle Safety
  Foundation (MSF)
2 Jenner St. Ste. 150
Irvine, CA 92718
949-727-3227
  (executive offices)
800-446-9227
  (course locations)
www.msf-usa.org
Hundreds of sites nationwide.

Motorcycle Safety Program
  Northern Illinois University
College of Continuing Ed.
DeKalb, IL 60115-2860
815-753-1683
www.online.niu.edu/mcycle

Rider Training (Cont'd)

Team Hammer
  Advanced Riding School
P.O. Box 183
Wildomar, CA 92595
909-245-6414
www.teamhammer.com

U.S. Women's Motocross
  League
P.O. Box 1674
Ramona, CA 92065
760-788-5277
wideopen@bendnet.com
www.wml-mx.com

3,000 members. Est. 1992. A non-profit organization"specializing in the promotion and development needs of the women's off-road competitive motorcycle market. WML serves as a clearinghouse for information . . . [and is] dedicated to serving female motocross athletes by offering training, media exposure, and growth programs."

SADDLEBAGS AND TANKBAGS

Chase Harper
P.O. Box 4098
Santa Barbara, CA 93140
805-965-7977
www.chaseharper.com

Givi Luggage Systems
805 Pressley Rd. Ste. 101
Charlotte, NC 28217
877-679-GIVI
www.givi.it

S&S Cycle & Supply
304 Rolling Trail
Amarillo, TX 79108
806-355-8541
800-321-2735

Eclipse
3771 E. Ellsworth Rd.
Ann Arbor, MI 48108
313-971-5552
800-666-1500
www.eclipselugggage.com

RKA
2175 Bluebell Dr.
Santa Rosa, CA 95403
707-579-5045

SEATS

Corbin
11445 Commercial Pkwy.
Castroville, CA 95012
800-538-7035 (CA)
800-223-4332 (FL)
daytona@corbin.com

Hartco
P.O. Box 148
Satsuma, FL 31289
800-446-7772

LeMans
c/o Drag Specialties
P.O. Box 9336
Minneapolis, MN 55440
800-222-3400

Le Pera Enterprises
8207 Lankershim Blvd.
N. Hollywood, CA 91605
818-767-5110

Mustang
P.O. Box 29
Terryville, CT 06786
800-243-1392
www.mustangseats.com

Seats (Cont'd)

Russell Day Long Saddles
P.O. Box 609
Fall River Mills, CA 96028
916-336-5323
800-4-DAY-LONG
www.day-long.com

Sargent Cycle Upholstery
44 E. 1st St.
Jacksonville, FL 32206
904-354-4531
800-749-SEAT
www.sargeantcycle.com

Travelcade
17801 S. Susana Rd.
Rancho Dominguez, CA
  90221
310-638-1222
800-397-7709
www.saddlemen.com

SHOCK ABSORBERS AND LOWERING KITS

Fox Racing Shox
3641 Charter Park Dr.
San Jose, CA 95136
408-269-9201
www.foxracingshox.com

Hagon
c/o Quinn Motorcycles
335 Litchfield Turnpike
Bethany, CT 06524
203-393-2651
www.davequinnmotorcycle.com
For vintage bikes.

Koni America
8085 Production Ave.
Florence, KY 41042
606-727-5000
800-922-2616

Lindemann Engineering
520 McGlincey Ln. #3
Campbell, CA 95008
408-371-6151
www.lam-suspension.com

Marzocchi
c/o Cosmopolitan Motors
301 Jacksonville Rd.
Hatboro, PA 19040
215-672-9100
800-523-2522
www.cosmotor.com
Mostly dual-shocks.

Ohlins
c/o Noleen Racing
16276 Koala Rd.
Adelanto, CA 92301
619-246-5000

Progressive Suspension
11129 G Ave.
Hesperia, CA 92345
619-948-4012
www.progressivesuspension.com

George Quay's
3201 6th Ave.
Beaver Falls, PA 15010
724-846-9055
www.pro-action.com
Dirt bike specialists.

Race Tech Suspension
3227 Producer Way #127
Pomona, CA 91768
909-594-7755
www.race-tech.com

Shoc Connection
4680 Los Angeles Ave.
Simi Valley, CA 93063
805-584-2805
www.shocconnection.com

Too-Tech Racing
19333 Sturgess Dr.
Torrance, CA 90503
310-371-3887

White Brothers
24845 Corbit Pl.
Yorba Linda, CA 92687
714-692-3404

Works Performance
21045 Osbourne St.
Canoga Park, CA 91324
818-701-1010
www.worksperformance.com

SIDECARS AND TRAILERS

American Jawa Ltd.
See Jawa/MZ in MC
MANUFACTURERS.

California Sidecar/Escapade
  Trailer
100 Motorcycle Run
Arlington, VA 22922
804-263-6500
800-824-1523
www.californiasidecar.com

Chariot
3912 Tampa Rd.
Oldsmar, FL 34677
813-855-5801
www.chariot-trailer.com

Cycle Mate
102 Sagritta St.
Edgerton, MN 56128
800-643-6237
www.cycle-mate.com

Motorvation
941 Fourth Ave.
Sibley, IA 51249
712-754-3664
www.motorvation.com

See also United Sidecar Assn.
in CLUBS, *Hack'd* in
PERIODICALS.

TIRES

Avon
P.O. Box 336
Edmonds, WA 98020
206-771-2115
800-624-7470
www.avontires.com

Bridgestone/Firestone
1 Bridgestone Park
P.O. Box 140991
Nashville, TN 37214-0991
615-391-0088
800-543-7522
www.bridgestonefirestone.com

Cheng Shin (Maxxis)
545 Old Peachtree Rd.
Suwanee, GA 30174
770-962-5932
www.maxxistires.com

Continental
1800 Continental Blvd.
Charlotte, NC 28273
704-583-3900

Dunlop
P.O. Box 1109
Buffalo, NY 14240-1109
716-639-5200
www.dunloptire.com

IRC
30321 Whipple Rd.
Union City, CA 94587
510-441-0126
www.irc.com

Kenda USA
7095 Americana Pkwy.
Reynoldsburg, OH 43068
614-866-9803

Kings Tire USA
(Nichols Motorcycle Supply)
4135 W. 126 St.
Alsip, IL 60658
708-597-3340

Metzeler/Pirelli
300 N. Potts Town Pike #280
Exton, PA 19341
610-524-2190
800-722-3336
www.metzeler.com
www.pirelli.com

Michelin
P.O. Box 19001
Greenville, SC 29602-9001
803-458-5000
www.michelin.com

TOURING RESOURCES

Int'l Motorcycle Touring
  Council
9401 N. 7th Ave.
Phoenix, AZ 85021
602-943-9030
www.members.aol.com/imcta

Tour info worldwide.

Motorcycle Touring Assn. &
  Venture Touring Society
877-833-3687
www.vtsmta.com

Whiptail Motorcycle
  Adventures
P.O. Box 29831
Santa Fe, NM 87592-9831
505-474-8099
www.whiptailtours.com

"Women on Top of the
World" is a planned women-
only ride to Khardung La, the
highest motorable pass in the
Indian Himalayas.

WEB SITES AND PORTALS

Web Sites and Portals—Women's Interest

About.com
http://motorcycles.about.
  com/autos/motorcycles/
  msub3.htm

Use this URL (web address)
for some nice women's
motorcycling links.

American Borders
www.verbum.com/jaunt/
  borders/

Motojournalist Carla King's
travelogues from her North
American, Chinese, and Indian excursions.

Around the World
  Following the Sun
www.ardi.si/benka

Motojournalist Bernarda
"Benka" Pulko's dispatches
from her around-the-world
trek.

Bikerlady Worldwide
www.ladybiker.com

Chat, rider profiles, excellent
links for gear, etc., dozens of
women's personal home
pages.

Greasergrrls
www.greasergrrls.com

Cars and bikes: chat, book reviews, gallery, tech.

HearMeRoar.net
roarlives@att.net
www.hearmeroar.net

Author's website. Gallery including photos and notes not
found in this book, updates
on author's activities, great
links.

MotoDirectory.com
www.mshopper.eurografix.com/
  links/women.htm

Use this link for a great list of
women's clubs, apparel, and
dozens of female bikers' home
pages.

Motorradfahrerinnen
http://rover.mainz.netsurf
  .de/~uschla/bikefrauen.html

German with some English
pages. Profiles of female
global motorcycle adventurers
and other interesting items.

Ridin' the Wind
www.ridinthewind.com

Interactive site with international rider bios, chat, gallery
(with photos of women's tattoos), events, safety issues,
cybermall.

Web Sites and Portals—Women's Interest (Cont'd)

RoadDivas.com
  (a/k/a Bikerlady.com)
www.roaddivas.com
www.bikerlady.com
Sasha Mullins, Editor
sasha@ladybiker.net

An evolving networking portal and forum for riders, entrepreneurs, artists, and webmistresses.

Women in Sport
  Touring (WIST)
Kyrie Collins, Organizer
shenescrpr@aol.com
www.phippsytowers.cwc.net/
  wfpg.htm
archives: www.magpie.com/
  digests.html

News, tech advice, road tales, chat.

Web Sites and Portals—General

American Motorcycle
  Network
www.americanmotor.com

Industry news, events, products.

Motorcycle Reports
Ian Smith Information
P.O. Box 9440
Denver, CO 80209-0440
303-777-2385
www.mcreports.com

Reprints of magazine articles on most bikes from 1960–present.

Motorcycle Web Ring
www.geocities.com/
  motorcity/4700/

A collection of home pages and motorcycle sites that "strive to bring adventure, good information, and a good image to the sport of motorcycling."

www.motorcycleworld.com

A great all-around resource for new and used bike comparisons, club listings, motorcycle news, and events. It has a dealer locator and is a portal to *CyberCycle* magazine.

Related Sites and Organizations

American Woman
  Motorscene
800-523-9737
Courtney Caldwell, Pub.
courtney
  @americanwomanmag.com
www.americanwomanmag.
  com

Mostly cars but still retains some motorcycling. Evolved from the print publication *American Woman MotorSports,* which began as *American Woman Road Rider.*

Woman Motorist
www.womanmotorist.com

Mostly cars, but has motorcycle reviews and events.

Related Sites and Organizations (Cont'd)

Women's Sports Foundation
wosport@aol.com
www.
   womenssportsfoundation.org

WWWomen's Sports
   Webring
http://wwwomen.com/
   webring/webring_sports.htm

Started in 1996 to link
women's sports content on
the web.

WINDSHIELDS AND FAIRINGS

Aeroflow
P.O. Box 11990
Costa Mesa, CA 92627
714-557-3119
For BMWs.

Clearview Shields
59113 Hwy. 285
P.O. Box 747
Bailey, CO 80421
800-798-6089
Custom-built shields.

Memphis Shades
158 Mills St.
Collierville, TN 38017
901-853-0293
www.memphisshades.com

National Cycle
P.O. Box 158
Maywood, IL 60153-0158
708-343-0400
www.nationalcycle.com

Parabellum
82 Spring Rd.
Dahlonega, GA 30533
706-864-8051
www.parabellum.com
For BMWs.

Rifle
3140 El Camino Real
Atascadero, CA 93422
800-262-1237 (USA)
800-663-1016 (CAN)
www.rifle.com

Saeng TA
P.O. Box 1246
Columbus, NE 68602
800-TOURING
402-563-3444
www.saeng.com
Winglets and adhesive edging
to redirect turbulence.

Slipstreamer
10820 Mankato St. NE
Blaine, MN 55449
612-780-9757
www.slipstreamer.com

Swanee/Pacifico
1550 S. Main
Milton Freewater, OR 97862
503-938-6174
800-547-8273

ACKNOWLEDGMENTS

I'd like to thank my inspirations—all the great women motorcyclists who gave their time and energy to participate in this book. Most especially I'd like to thank my "Charter Girls"—the women who, starting in the spring of 1990, were with me as I began this long journey of writing and riding: Becky Brown, Sandy Couture, Patty Mills, Dot Robinson, Jo Giovannoni, Courtney Caldwell, Fran Crane, Pam Cummings, Nancy Delgado, Amy Mullins, Catharine Rambeau, and Bessie Stringfield. These women—and others too many to name!—shared their lives through words, photographs, and hospitality during repeated interviews over the years. A project of this scope relies also on networking. Many women recommended other great riders.

How do I adequately thank the love of my life, my husband, Frank Dusek? The moment we first laid eyes on each other at a vintage bike show, when I parked my motorcycle on soft grass, he knelt down to wedge a support under my kickstand to prevent my bike from sinking. After that day, he became my greatest support and has—in ways too numerous to count—prevented *me* from sinking. I could not have finished the book without his unwavering love, friendship, and encouragement. Many parts of the Resource Directory were updated through Frank's efforts.

And how do I adequately thank my mother, Marie Ferrar? Mom has been a tremendous help in every way that a mother could be. Among other tasks, my mother transcribed endless hours of interview tapes.

We are saddened that my beloved father Anthony was not among us to see the results.

My friend Nelly Edmondson-Gupta was the first person to lay eyes on the draft. Nelly's insight helped me see with clarity what I needed to submit to Crown (my first publisher), and what I didn't. Like me, Nelly had once been a full-time freelance writer who toughed it in the toughest city on earth, New York, and she *understood everything* I went through. My other friends, including Joanne Flaster, Barbara Giannoccaro, and Inez Boyce, my wonderful, creative aunt, lent their ears and much encouragement.

My gratitude goes to Sharon Squibb, my editor at Crown, and Patricia Haskell, my former literary agent, for their early efforts on behalf of me and the book. Laura Brengelman and Kim Brittenham encouraged me to get the rights back from Crown, and they both provided valuable feedback on the book's new Resource Directory. Many thanks go to them, and to my new publishers, Dan and Judy Kennedy of Whitehorse Press, and to editor Lisa Dionne.

Several key people and companies supported me in a variety of ways, including Steve Piehl and Martin Jack Rosenblum of the Harley-Davidson Motor Company, who arranged for me to reprint photos from H-D's Juneau Avenue Archives. Thanks to Kal Demitros of H-D, without whom I could never have made it to Sturgis in 1990.

I am grateful to BMW of North America, which has been supportive through the efforts of Scott Arigot and, years ago, Carla Harmon. My gratitude goes to Beverly St. Clair-Baird of Discover Today's Motorcycling, and Ed Youngblood, former president of the American Motorcyclist Association.

Special thanks to Denney Colt for riding to Jones Beach on a chilly November day to have her photo taken for the cover. Thanks also to Kathy Heller, Debbie Matthews, Elaine Ruff, Tami Rice, Sue Slate, Gin Shear, Patti Carpenter, Rudy and Anne Tully Ruderman, Dee Modglin, Jacqui Sturgess, and Gasper Trama.

To the motorcycle community, I say "thanks for the memories." I met so many diverse people whom I would never have otherwise encountered. People who at first were complete strangers opened their homes to me when I needed places to stay during my journeys. I made some friendships that will last a lifetime, and I retain some priceless, and humorous, memories of encounters on the road.

One such was the summer afternoon in 1993 when I met Rusty Dennis, the woman portrayed by Cher in the film *Mask*. Rusty said, "I'll take ya to the clubhouse and introduce ya to some folks that the movie characters were based on." I didn't know what to expect of a 1%er clubhouse in Southern California. Inside, all I saw were a couple of folks chatting and a sign that warned, THROWING BUTTS ON THE FLOOR COULD BE CAUSE FOR YOU TO LEAVE.

Rusty blurted, "Where's the depravity?"

Best of all was the weekend in July of '93, which I spent with eighty-year-old Vera Griffin. Her legacy lives in the stories and vintage photographs of herself and other Motor Maids, which she shared for this book. To get through a construction zone filled with rattlesnakes, Vera rode with her feet up on the handlebars. Some tough cookie, this lady was.

In my working travels, I wanted to meet as many women as possible and spend as much time as possible with each one. To cover miles quickly, I rode the superslabs. As I was packing my bike to leave Vera's, I confessed that at interstate speeds, my bubble-shaped windshield directed turbulence at my head and caused an awful wind roar inside my helmet. Earplugs were no match for this.

For a second, Vera contemplated the difficulty I must be having riding a high-tech machine on paved roads. Then she said, "Powder puffs. Stuff 'em inside your helmet liner. Perhaps they will muffle the noise."

She rode with me to the border of her home state, Indiana, where we stopped at a strip-mall and bought the puffs. To the wide-eyed locals, we must have been as weird a sight in 1993 as the Van Buren sisters had been in 1916. Here was Vera, a senior citizen astride a Harley-Davidson Sportster. And here was me, a road-weary woman who could barely wedge her butt onto her saddle because the bike was piled so thoroughly with junk. And here we were, sitting in McDonald's, stuffing powder puffs in a motorcycle helmet.

We said good-bye and rode our separate ways. The puffs didn't work as hoped. I pulled off the interstate, pulled out my tool kit, and removed the evil windshield. Then I pulled out a map, followed it to the nearest squiggly line, and remembered why I loved riding in the first place.

NOTES

INTRODUCTION

1. "My Mother the Motorcyclist" copyright 1978 Anne Tully Ruderman (unpublished).

CHAPTER ONE

1. From a letter to *Harley Women* magazine, November/December 1993.

2. Kolb wrote *On the Perimeter* with Bill Stermer (New London, MO: Maverick, 1983).

3. From a letter to *Women on Wheels* magazine, September/October 1994.

CHAPTER TWO

1. Frances E. Willard, *A Wheel Within a Wheel* (1895).

2. Frederick A. Talbot, "Across America by Motor-Cycle: A Four-Thousand Mile Race Against Time," *Wide World,* American Edition (1906). W. C. Chadeayne was said to be the second man to cross the continent by motorcycle.

3. Bob Carpenter, et al., "The History of Women in Motorcycling," *Road Rider* magazine, July 1985 and July 1990. These articles formed the basis of "Women in Motorcycling," the 1990 inaugural exhibit at the American Motorcyclist Association's Heritage Museum.

4. *Second to None: A Documentary History of American Women,* edited by Ruth Barnes Moynihan, Cynthia Russert, and Laurie Crumpacker (University of Nebraska Press, 1993).

5. Betty Friedan wrote about her suburban, prefeminist lifestyle in *It Changed My Life* (New York: W. W. Norton, 1976).

6. Bob Carpenter, et al., op. cit.

7. Bob and Patti Carpenter, "Theresa Wallach: A Brief Biography and Interview with One of Motorcycling's Most Remarkable Women," *Road Rider,* Vol. 8, No. 4, April 1977.

8. Ibid. copyright *Road Rider.* Reprinted with permission.

9. Gill's story ran in *The Enthusiast* in January 1994.

CHAPTER THREE

1. Susan J. Douglas, *Where the Girls Are: Growing Up Female with the Mass Media* (New York: Times Books, 1994).

2. "The Female Factor: Mr. Cheap Tour Has a Problem with Girls," *Cycle,* April 1988.

3. From the AMA Heritage Museum's "Women in Motorcycling" exhibit.

4. Tommy Sandham, *The Castrol Book of the Scottish Six Days Trial* (Somerset, U.K.: Haynes, 1982).

5. Gail Sheehy, *Passages: Predictable Crises of Adult Life* (New York: Bantam, 1977).

6. *Harley Women,* November/December 1990.

7. Billye Nipper, "Maybe Rodney Dangerfield Should Ride a Motorcycle—I Get a Lot of Respect," *Women on Wheels,* July/August 1991.

CHAPTER FOUR

1. Ann-Margret with Todd Gold, *Ann-Margret: My Story* (New York: G. P. Putnam's Sons, 1994).

2. Caressa French, *Hog Heaven* (Freedom, CA: Crossing Press, 1994).

3. Woody Hockswender, "Born to Be Wild, but Feminine," *The New York Times,* July 16, 1991.

4. John Marchese, "Forever Harley," *The New York Times,* October 17, 1993.

5. Ann-Margret, *Ann-Margret.*

6. According to a long-term participant-observation study, "Women in Outlaw Motorcycle Gangs," by Columbus B. Hopper and Johnny Moore, published in the *Journal of Contemporary Ethnography,* January 4, 1990.

CHAPTER FIVE

1. Race officials disagreed with the cause of the accident, claiming there was no oil.

CHAPTER SIX

1. Male road racers are often husbands and fathers. Over the decades, a few men have suffered disabling injuries and a few have died. At this writing, there were no reported incidents of permanent disability or death among female road racers in this country. Some would argue that women race more conservatively than men, thus lowering their risks.

CHAPTER SEVEN

1. Chris Kallfelz, "Class of '94—Loretta Lynn's: The Past, Present and Future of Motocross," *American Motorcyclist,* November 1994.

2. Mariah Burton Nelson, *The Stronger Women Get, the More Men Love Football—Sexism and the American Culture of Sports* (New York: Harcourt Brace, 1994).

CHAPTER TEN

1. Lawrence Grodsky, "Stayin' Safe: Gender Bender," *Rider,* October 1992.

CHAPTER ELEVEN

1. The full title of the study is *Motorcycle Accident Cause Factors and Identification of Countermeasures,* by Dr. Harry Hurt, et al.

2. In 1993, there were 2,400 fatalities. Nearly half of all fatalities are among riders under age 25. Friday-night crashes are three times more likely to be lethal.

3. From the *Experienced RiderCourse Participant Handbook* (Irvine, CA: Motorcycle Safety Foundation, 1992). Reprinted with permission.

INDEX

ABOUT THE AUTHOR

Ann Ferrar is an award-winning journalist whose career has spanned more than two decades. She has written creative non-fiction in multiple media, on subjects ranging from health and women's issues, to music and motorcycling. In 1992, she was recognized with three awards for her writing of public health education materials for the March of Dimes Birth Defects Foundation. In 1997, she received the American Motorcyclist Association Hazel Kolb Brighter Image Award, for *Hear Me Roar's* positive impact on the motorcycling community and on the public.

Ferrar has lectured at universities and libraries for Women's History Month, and has served as an advisor to museum curators and filmmakers on women's motorcycling history. She has appeared in the international television documentary *The Secret History of Bikers* and in CNN's *All About Women.* Photographs from Ferrar's *Hear Me Roar* collection have appeared in the Field Museum of Chicago's exhibit of *The Art of the Motorcycle,* and her ideas have helped to enhance the AMA's expanded *Women & Motorcycling* exhibit.

To research, write and photograph *Hear Me Roar,* Ferrar rode 30,000 miles solo to interview hundreds of women bikers, explore historical archives, and attend motorcycle events. To date, *Hear Me Roar* is the first and only book of its kind in the Library of Congress. Ferrar's efforts were richly rewarded by universal critical acclaim for the book. *Hear Me Roar* was hailed by the *New York Times* as "a woman's symphony on the road," by *Thunder Press* and *Woman Rider* as "the bible of women's motorcycling," by dozens of other publications worldwide, and by riders and industry leaders of both genders.

Ferrar has been involved in motorcycling for more than 20 years and began riding her own bike in 1990. Since then, she has owned six motorcycles. She pursues her career as a non-fiction writer specializing in consumer health, patient education and women's issues, writing for the Internet, video, and print media. A native of New York City, Ferrar lives on Long Island with her husband, Frank Dusek, who is also a biker and book-lover.